Updated for 9th Printing

GPS
Now with
GPS Waypoints

ARIZONA GHOST TOWNS AND MINING CAMPS

Text by Philip Varney

Photographs by *Arizona Highways* Contributors

ARIZONA HIGHWAYS

(Front Cover)
Vestiges of settlements, such as
these at Pearce, speak of the
fleeting nature of many mining
ventures.
JERRY JACKA

(Inside Front Cover)
The Vulture Mine's assay
office, built in 1884, contained
living quarters.
JOHN DREW

Book Design: Gary Bennett
Cover Design: Ronda Johnson
Color Photography Editor: Richard Maack
Historical Photograph Research: Dean Smith
Production Assistants: Annette Phares, Diana Benzel-Rice and Vicky Snow
Regional Maps: ADOT Photogrammetry and Mapping Division

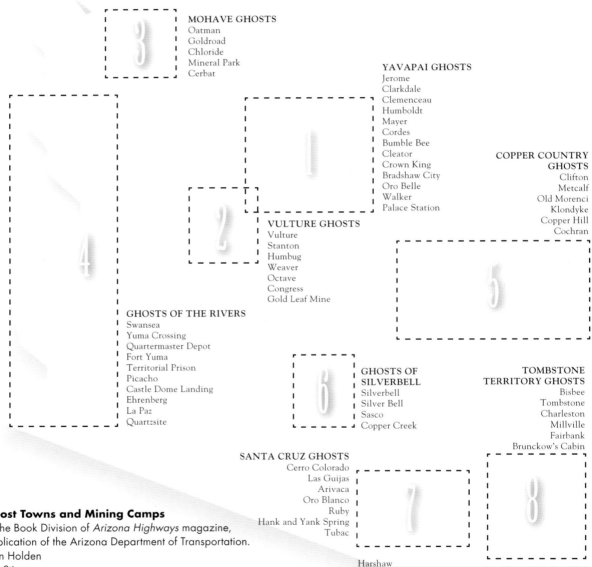

MOHAVE GHOSTS
Oatman
Goldroad
Chloride
Mineral Park
Cerbat

YAVAPAI GHOSTS
Jerome
Clarkdale
Clemenceau
Humboldt
Mayer
Cordes
Bumble Bee
Cleator
Crown King
Bradshaw City
Oro Belle
Walker
Palace Station

COPPER COUNTRY GHOSTS
Clifton
Metcalf
Old Morenci
Klondyke
Copper Hill
Cochran

VULTURE GHOSTS
Vulture
Stanton
Humbug
Weaver
Octave
Congress
Gold Leaf Mine

GHOSTS OF THE RIVERS
Swansea
Yuma Crossing
Quartermaster Depot
Fort Yuma
Territorial Prison
Picacho
Castle Dome Landing
Ehrenberg
La Paz
Quartzsite

GHOSTS OF SILVERBELL
Silverbell
Silver Bell
Sasco
Copper Creek

TOMBSTONE TERRITORY GHOSTS
Bisbee
Tombstone
Charleston
Millville
Fairbank
Brunckow's Cabin

SANTA CRUZ GHOSTS
Cerro Colorado
Las Guijas
Arivaca
Oro Blanco
Ruby
Hank and Yank Spring
Tubac

Harshaw
Mowry
Washington Camp
Duquesne
Lochiel
Sunnyside
Salero
Alto
Helvetia
Kentucky Camp

Fort Bowie
Dos Cabezas
Cochise
Dragoon Springs
Pearce
Courtland
Gleeson

Arizona Ghost Towns and Mining Camps

Prepared by the Book Division of *Arizona Highways* magazine,
a monthly publication of the Arizona Department of Transportation.
Publisher: Win Holden
Editor: Robert Stieve
Managing Editor/Books: Kelly Vaughn Kramer
Photography Editor: Jeff Kida
Production Director: Michael Bianchi
Production Coordinator: Annette Phares

Website: www.arizonahighways.com

Library of Congress Number 93-73449   ISBN-13: 978-1-932082-46-3

Contents

3

Introduction

etting to know Arizona intimately takes one onto the land itself. Histories, magazines, or Western pulp novels cannot begin to tell the whole story. To love this remarkable state is to explore its canyons, photograph its diverse flora and fauna, and admire and respect the ways of its native people.

To delve into why settlers came to this unforgiving but spectacular land, we need only begin with its name. "Arizona" appears in Spanish writings beginning in the 1730s, referring to a ranch that now would be in Mexico. The area around Arizona (a name perhaps from a Basque term for "good oaks," perhaps from an Indian word for "small springs" or "place of little water") was important to the Spaniards because of its silver.

Its wealth of gold, silver, and copper transformed Arizona into a territory and, eventually, a state. Prospectors in the 1860s, fanning eastward after the great Gold Rush in California, found silver south of Tucson, in new claims and in old Spanish and Mexican workings. They found placer deposits and gold lodes near the confluence of the Colorado and Gila rivers. And finally, adventurers discovered gold in the hills near what is now Prescott. These prospectors attracted miners (there is a difference), who ushered in merchants, saloonkeepers, clergymen, lawmakers, and law-breakers — bringing the white man's civilization to the Arizona Territory.

All communities of importance in early Arizona were related to mining. River towns sent supplies to miners. Forts protected them. Farmers fed them. Eventually, railroads carried their ore to market and brought goods from around the world to their hometowns.

Arizona's history is most clearly illustrated by the quest for its mineral wealth. The state seal depicts a miner with a pick and shovel. The state motto is "Ditat Deus" ("God enriches"— referring to the state's natural resources). Influential legislators, lawyers, bankers, doctors, judges, and soldiers all had ties — directly or indirectly — to the mining industry.

To experience this mining history one can explore its remnants, the ghost towns and mining camps that were left behind when the riches faded. Of those communities that remain, most have only a reminder or two to prove they existed. A few have significant structures and mining evidence, and a handful thrive even though their mines closed long ago.

By my definition, a ghost town has two characteristics: The population has decreased markedly, and the initial reason for its settlement (such as a mine or a railroad) no longer keeps people in the community. A ghost town can be

(Above) *To carry workers back to the Monica Mine after wild weekends, Charles Evans stacked iron bunk beds on his freight wagon, c. 1910.* DESERT CABALLEROS WESTERN MUSEUM
(Right) *The expression "two bits" comes from the "bit," a 12.5-cent coin issued by saloons and cigar makers.* SHARLOT HALL MUSEUM
(Facing Page) *J.W. Swart's Saloon in Charleston, 1885.* ARIZONA HISTORICAL SOCIETY

completely deserted, like Swansea, Courtland, or Copper Hill; it can have a few residents, like Gleeson, Stanton, or Cleator; or it can have genuine signs of vitality like Crown King, Oatman, and Cochise. Remember, however, that some "signs of vitality" may change: The hours of operation of a lonely outpost in a remote ghost town when you visit may have altered from the information in this book; perhaps the business will even be closed.

It can be argued that the great mining towns of Bisbee, Tombstone, and Clifton are too alive to be included in a ghost town book. Still, even a town like Bisbee has "ghost town" indicators: Its population dropped from 35,000 to 6,000; the mines are closed; several schools no longer have students; many stores are shuttered.

Why are so many people fascinated by ghost towns? Mystery writer Tony Hillerman, in a foreword to one of my previous books on ghost towns, put it perfectly: "To me, to many of my friends, to scores of thousands of Americans, these ghost towns offer a sort of touching-place with the past. We stand in their dust and try to project our imagination backward into what they were long ago. Now and then, if the mood and the light, and the weather are exactly right, we almost succeed."

Please remember that ghost towns are fragile places. My photograph of the school at Sunnyside (p. 113) may have been the last ever taken of it standing. A few months after I took the picture, the building collapsed. One can only hope that it was from its own weight of over 90 years, and not the push of a thoughtless vandal. Our "touching-places with the past" are to be protected and treasured as well as explored and photographed.

Philip Varney

(Far Left) *The clubhouse for Congress Mine executives, c. 1898.*
<small>DESERT CABALLEROS WESTERN MUSEUM</small>
(Left) *Light in the mines, in early days, was often provided by candleholders*
that could be stuck into timbers, set on ledges, or wedged into cracks.
<small>JOHN DREW</small>
(Below) *A five-foot vein of argentiferrous galena (silver and lead),*
at the 500-foot level of Tombstone Consolidated Mines Co., c. 1904.
<small>ARIZONA HISTORICAL SOCIETY</small>

CHAPTER 1

Yavapai Ghosts

With its tree-shaded courthouse square, historic Whiskey Row, stately Victorian homes, and often-overlooked old Fort Whipple, Prescott, the seat of Yavapai County, is a refreshing retreat. Founded in 1864 and named for historian William H. Prescott, the town served as Arizona's first territorial capital. The governor's home still stands on the grounds of the Sharlot Hall Museum, which houses some of Arizona's best and most informative historical exhibits.

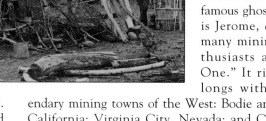

The lure of mineral wealth brought the first white settlers to the area. When gold was found in 1863 in the mountains to the southeast along Lynx Creek, a rush resulted. Settlers named the surrounding mountains the Bradshaws for William D. Bradshaw, who, along with his brother Isaac, found gold not long after the Lynx Creek strike.

For the ghost town buff, Yavapai County features more than a dozen sites (including four featured in Chapter Two). A group of mining camps is located along a road that parallels the old railroad that once connected Prescott to the Bradshaw Mountains. For part of the trip, the back-roads traveler ascends the old right of way of that "Impossible Railroad" to the mining camp of Crown King. A side trip from Prescott ventures south along Walker Road and Senator Highway, the latter a dirt road that wouldn't qualify as a "highway" under any current definition. The roads lead to two historic gems: an 1880s charcoal kiln and an 1875 stagecoach station.

But the area's most famous ghost town by far is Jerome, described by many mining camp enthusiasts as "The Big One." It rightfully belongs with other legendary mining towns of the West: Bodie and Columbia, California; Virginia City, Nevada; and Cripple Creek and Central City, Colorado.

Jerome is Arizona's most dramatic, most extensive ghost town.

(Above) In 1863, when the Joseph Walker party discovered gold in Lynx Creek near the future site of Prescott, jubilant miners hastily built shacks such as this one with little concern for architectural niceties.
SHARLOT HALL MUSEUM
(Facing Page) Now providing apartments and business space, the Central Hotel building in Jerome was erected in 1905 and renovated in the early 1920s.
PHILIP VARNEY

9

Jerome and Clarkdale

Jerome is unique. While other mining camps cluster in canyons, huddle at the bases of hills, or stand along silvery creeks, Jerome clings precariously to the side of a mountain, seemingly defying gravity. If you glimpse it from the east, it begins as a glint of roofs in the sun, perched impossibly high on a distant hill. If you come from the west over Mingus Mountain, Jerome materializes suddenly, appearing to cascade down the 30-percent grade of Cleopatra Hill.

This is not a ghost town to be sampled in an hour, although one might get a taste of it in that time. I have prowled Jerome's central city, back streets, museums, shops, and ruins in visits spanning 30 years — and each time I discover a building, a fact, an enchantment that had eluded me.

Clarkdale, less than 5 miles away but almost 2,000 feet below Jerome, is often overlooked by those bewitched by the distant sighting of its more famous neighbor. But Clarkdale's history is also tied to the wealth of Cleopatra Hill. And the town has many reminders of its past.

The colorful mineral deposits of Mingus Mountain, Woodchute Mountain, and Cleopatra Hill, collectively called the Black Hills, were used by the Sinagua Indians who lived nearby more than 1,000 years ago at what has become Tuzigoot National Monument. The Sinagua favored beautiful blue azurite, a basic carbonate of copper. When they came through in the 1500s, the Spaniards dismissed the area's abundant copper deposits. They sought gold.

Jerome was built on the most level spot on Cleopatra Hill. Nevertheless, this 1910 view clearly shows the effects of erosion caused by the steep grade and extensive mining activity.
Jerome State Historic Park

Copper became an important commodity with the advent of the Industrial Revolution. Morris Andrew Ruffner found a promising deposit in 1876 and filed two claims. Unable to finance a mining operation, he sought the assistance of two brothers, Angus and John McKinnon, giving them a two-thirds interest in his claims. Within four years the McKinnons were anxious to get out of a partnership that seemed to be going nowhere and forced a sale.

Eastern entrepreneurs sent metallurgist and copper specialist Dr. James Douglas, who was to become famous in Arizona mining history, to evaluate the potential of the claims. Douglas found the ore body promising but balked at its incredibly remote location. His recommendation: Don't invest.

Frederick F. Thomas and Territorial Governor Frederick Augustus Tritle wanted to buy out the Ruffner-McKinnon claims, but needed Eastern capital to do it. In 1882 they collected a group of investors that included Eugene Murray Jerome, a young successful New York attorney, and founded the United Verde Copper Company. Jerome became secretary-treasurer of the company, and Arizona's most famous copper town became his namesake. What piqued the investors' interest was the completion in 1882 of the Atlantic and Pacific Railroad, which shortened the distance from mine to railroad to a mere 60 miles. Before the Atlantic and Pacific, the nearest railhead to Jerome had been at Abilene, Kansas.

The United Verde was sold again in 1888 to William Andrews Clark, a consummate financier from Montana. By age 40 he was a millionaire three times over. He once boasted he would be the richest man in Montana and one of its U.S. senators. Thirteen years after purchasing the United Verde, he was both.

During the early days of Clark's ownership, the mine "seemed to become richer with each dig," according to one report. Despite the mine's success, Jerome's early days were not without problems. The town was built on the most level spot on Cleopatra Hill, but that put it close to the smelter's choking sulfurous smoke. Vegetation on the hill virtually disappeared; the water supply was questionable. As an obituary in the *Jerome Chronicle* reported, one Hugh Caddell "drank from the waters of Bitter Creek and never was himself again."

A drop in copper prices in 1891 required a reduction in the cost of getting ore to market. A railway connection with the cross-country line was essential. The resulting United Verde and Pacific Railway had 186 curves and was described as the "crookedest line in the world."

Although the ore body proved to be exceedingly rich, a fire that started in the upper levels of the mine in 1894 forced a change in the way ore was retrieved. Because of

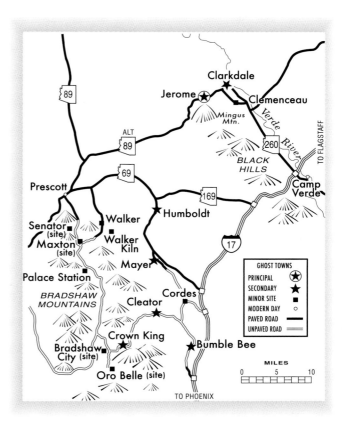

intense heat and the danger of cave-ins, the mine, which had been producing an astonishing 3 million pounds of copper per month, could no longer be worked by underground methods.

The solution was to remove the smelter from directly above the mine fire (which burned, amazingly, for 33 years) and switch to open-pit mining. This required a new railroad and huge tracts of land for a replacement smelter and its slag pile — as well as the vast sums of money to purchase them.

This infusion of capital had an enormous effect on Jerome, causing it to become a city of permanence and character. Despite fires in three successive years starting in 1897, each reincarnation of the town was an improvement upon the last. In 1900, Jerome — population 2,861 — was the fourth-largest city in the Arizona Territory. Residents came from England, Ireland, Mexico, China, Yugoslavia, Russia, Italy, and Germany. The town featured every kind of business and profession imaginable, including the "oldest." In 1895 Madame Jennie Banters built a boudoir on Main Street and brought her "girls" to town. Miners commented that the city of Jerome now had *all* the essential services.

In 1905, however, these "essential" services took a backward turn. The town council banned women from saloons, and marshal Fred Hawkins embarked on a futile campaign to close down Jerome's numerous opium dens.

Also in that year, William A. Clark, by then a U.S. senator from Montana, commissioned a magnificent private Pullman railroad car so he could travel the country in a style befitting one of the world's richest men. To cater to the necessities of such a personage, Clark was accompanied by a secretary, a valet, a cook, and a waiter.

In 1912 Arizona became the 48th state. That year also brought the introduction of open-pit mining in Jerome, which led to the construction of Clarkdale, a $2 million smelter town. The homes of upper management and a school were built on the hill closest to Jerome. Nearby, the business district featured municipal and commercial buildings. These two areas were collectively known as "Uptown" and were far removed from a series of blue-collar workers' homes situated down the hill. Across a draw nearer the smelter was "Patio Town," a euphemism for Mexican Town. It consisted of subsistence housing and was located outside Clarkdale's planned area.

Clarkdale has been eulogized as the apex of company towns. Books and articles emphasize William Clark's generosity and concern for his workers. Authors point to the housing, hospitals, and schools he built and to such Clarkdale amenities as swimming pools, tennis courts, clubhouses, and a golf course. But Patricia Paylore, who grew up in Clarkdale during the boom years, recalled that there was no library, no theater, and no forgetting the company's presence. She remembered unsupervised Patio Town as "the most human and enchanting place of all," a place where not just Mexicans but "strong-minded Gringos" preferred to live. She also recalled that nearby Cottonwood "was a 'free' town, unencumbered by Company restrictions, and its attraction for us resided in the adventure of seeing how other people lived."

Up in Jerome a rival to the United Verde, known as the United Verde Extension Mining Company (UVX), hit a fabulous body of ore in 1916. The mine was called the Little Daisy and proved to be worth $132 million.

United Verde Extension was under the management and part ownership of James S. Douglas II, son of the man who, in 1880, had advised people not to invest in Cleopatra Hill. The younger Douglas, later known as "Rawhide Jimmy," built his mansion and the $200,000 Little Daisy Hotel, named in honor of the mine, on opposite sides of the main shaft. The hotel was intended for miners, but its luxury made them feel uncomfortable: One miner complained there was no place to spit. White-collar workers and traveling businessmen became the occupants.

In the interim, the smelter at Clarkdale was fired up in 1915 and open-pit mining geared up for production. All did not go smoothly, however. Jerome was rocked by labor disputes in 1917. The Industrial Workers of the World (I.W.W. or "Wobblies") were competing with another union, and a strike resulted. Many in Jerome considered the I.W.W. group radical, revolutionary, and un-American. On July 10, some 250 men gathered at City

(**Above**) *The former Douglas mansion, now Jerome State Historic Park, is crowded with informative displays and memorabilia.*
PHILIP VARNEY
(**Left**) *Jerome provided many amenities in 1910 — ladies' finery in the New York Store, feed for horses, and all kinds of mining supplies. When fires periodically razed the business district, merchants stubbornly rebuilt it.*
SHARLOT HALL MUSEUM

Hall for "clean-up duty." They raided I.W.W. headquarters, rooming houses, and even private homes in search of strikers. More than 60 men were loaded into a cattle car and sent out of town. Some of the strikers ended up in jail in Prescott; others found themselves in Needles, California. The Jerome Deportation was a precursor of bigger things: Within a week, similar action on a far larger scale took place in Bisbee (see p. 120).

Nevertheless, by 1918 the open-pit mine was in full production. The timing couldn't have been better for Jerome. World War I dramatically increased the demand for copper — and increased its prices.

Production was augmented by the use of the monstrous Marion 300, a rail-mounted, full-revolving, coal-powered shovel developed for construction of the Panama Canal. Procured for the open-pit operation on a priority basis for the war effort, the Marion 300 was used until 1926, when it hit an unexploded dynamite charge, killing the operator and injuring several miners.

That also was the year William Andrews Clark died. His son, Charles, became president of United Verde until his death in 1933. Charles' brother, William A. Clark, Jr., succeeded him but died within the year. His son, W.A. Clark III, took the reins but was killed in a 1935 Verde Valley plane crash. That year the daughters of the family decided to sell the United Verde Copper Company to the Phelps Dodge Corporation for $20.8 million. Phelps Dodge then purchased the United Verde Extension from the Douglas family and a third company, the Verde Central Mine, bringing their total investment in Jerome to $35 million.

It was money well spent. By 1940, with the world again heading into war, Phelps Dodge had recovered its initial investment. At that point, three of the largest copper-producing areas in Arizona — Bisbee (see p. 116), Clifton-Morenci (see p. 82), and Jerome — were all owned by Phelps Dodge.

The UVX Mine closed in 1938. The United Verde continued producing until 1953, the year the Jerome Historical Society formed to make certain "America's Largest Ghost City" would be preserved and protected.

That ghost city would have been considerably larger if underground explosions and fault shifts hadn't caused many buildings to slide downhill, resulting in dozens of structures being razed from the 1930s into the '50s. At one point, two entire city blocks were destroyed.

Supposedly, residents became so accustomed to ground movement that one night, when a movie theater slipped two feet, the projector kept right on whirring, and the audience continued to watch in rapt attention, the movie being the only real excitement. Jerome's enterprising Chamber of Commerce gleefully advertised that it was "A town on the move!"

Today, in addition to being a photographer's paradise, Jerome has shops to browse, streets to wander, and two museums to examine. The museum operated by the

(Above) *The huge rail-mounted Marion shovel, used in digging the Panama Canal, helped excavate the United Verde's open-pit mine, gulping 8 cubic yards of earth with each bite. It was destroyed in 1926 when it bit into a buried dynamite charge.*
JEROME STATE HISTORIC PARK

(Right) *Jerome's Main Street harbors much history, including venerable buildings and exhibits in the Jerome Historical Society's Mine Museum, and many intriguing shops.* PHILIP VARNEY

Jerome Historical Society stands in the middle of town. It is crowded with informative displays and memorabilia. The other museum, the former Douglas mansion, is now Jerome State Historic Park. It contains one exhibit that leaves me awestruck every time I see it: a glass-enclosed model showing Jerome's incredible maze of underground shafts, tunnels, and railroads. A second city lived underneath the town.

On the road to the Douglas mansion stands the "Powderbox Church," so called because of the materials used in its construction. It was erected in 1939 as the "Mexican Methodist" church, an architectural imitation of Haven Methodist up on the hill. On the same road as the Powderbox Church is the shell of the Little Daisy Hotel, which was stripped for salvage in 1938 but has since been partially restored as a residence. Both are on private property.

Many buildings of historical significance stand in the central business district. An excellent way to get an overall view of Jerome is to take a walking tour of downtown. Then step into the Holy Family Catholic Church before continuing up the street to its end to view the open-pit mine gouged by the Marion 300 shovel. You might also want to hike the one-way back street behind the once-elegant homes of the company elite to the United Verde Hospital, the surgeon's clubhouse (itself a former hospital), and the old United Verde Apartments, before returning to Main Street (allow 30 minutes).

The Jerome Cemetery is worth a visit, too. As State Route 89A hairpins downhill past the old Jerome Union High School, turn left onto a dirt road and travel a short distance. The cemetery features markers for people who

(Above, Left) *Pastor Sabino Gonzalez stands before Jerome's fabled Powderbox Church, which he fashioned from discarded dynamite boxes and mine timbers for his Mexican Methodist congregation. His flock dwindled to seven in 1952, when this picture was taken, and he sadly locked the door.*
ART CLARK
(Above, Right) *Clarkdale's Patio Town, largely Hispanic, had a unique character unhampered by company restrictions.*
PHILIP VARNEY
(Right) *Many Mexican miners in Jerome lived in "The Gulch," shown in this 1954 photo.*
ART CLARK

came from all over the world to tap Jerome's riches. It also offers stunning views of Jerome, Clarkdale, Cottonwood, and the red cliffs of Sedona.

In the 1970s Clarkdale was almost a ghost town itself. Now the town is very much alive. An enormous cement plant west of town employs many of Clarkdale's citizens, and the town has attracted many retirees. Before crossing the bridge en route to Patio Town and the smelter ruins, you'll pass Clarkdale's biggest tourist attraction, the Verde Canyon Railroad. Once Clarkdale's link to the main Santa Fe line and the world's copper markets, this historic railroad passes along the banks of the Verde River and through beautiful canyons. In the old days, the trains primarily hauled copper out and brought supplies in, but it was also used by kids who would catch free rides, letting the conductor know where they wanted to get off for picnics and swimming. Later they would hail the engineer for a ride back to town.

South of Clarkdale is a ghost town from a much earlier era, Tuzigoot National Monument, a Sinagua Indian pueblo which flourished 1000 years ago. On the way to the monument, just after crossing the Verde River, a road to the left leads to the Clark mansion, which now stands in regal solitude on private property.

A final attraction that deserves mention is the Clemenceau Heritage Museum, at 1 N. Willard Street in Cottonwood. It is located in the 1924 Clemenceau School built by the United Verde Extension Copper Company. Now absorbed by the town of Cottonwood, Clemenceau was the site of the UVX smelter. The town was named in honor of Georges Clemenceau, French premier during World War I. The museum, operated by the Verde Historical Society, opened in 1991. At this writing, a vintage classroom and an extensive HO-scale model railroad of the Verde Valley are on permanent display, with two larger rooms used for temporary exhibits. (928) 634-2868.

Jerome, Clarkdale, and Clemenceau are monuments to Arizona's mineral wealth and its importance to our developing nation. Verde Valley mines have provided more than $2 billion in copper, an essential element in practically every modern convenience. The mines also produced $60 million in silver and $50 million in gold.

WHEN YOU GO: Jerome and Clarkdale are about 33 miles northeast of Prescott along State Route 89A, or about 115 miles north of Phoenix via Interstate 17 and state routes 260 and 89A.

From 1901-04 entrepreneur Frank Murphy built his "Impossible Railroad" from Mayer to the Bradshaw Mountain mining towns over terrain so steep that doubters said it couldn't be done. Lofty trestles, many switchbacks, and a tunnel had to be completed before standard-gauge tracks could be laid.
SHARLOT HALL MUSEUM

Murphy's Impossible Railroad

Prescott flourished in 1895. The recently completed Santa Fe, Prescott, and Phoenix Railroad linked central Arizona to the rest of the country. Gold deposits in the Bradshaw Mountains southeast of town were yielding $390,000 annually. And therein lies an interesting story.

To get the gold to a smelter, entrepreneur/mine owner/railroad president Frank Murphy proposed connecting the remote mountain sites by rail. In 1898 he completed the 26-mile, standard-gauge Prescott and Eastern Railroad to the mining and commercial center of Mayer, with an important stop at the smelter town of Humboldt.

But Murphy had much bigger plans. He envisioned extending the railroad some 25 miles from Mayer all the way to the Bradshaw Mountain Crown King mines. Since Crown King was almost 2,000 feet above Mayer and because of the steepness of the grade and the instability of the surface, naysayers derided the idea as "Murphy's Impossible Railroad."

Murphy advertised in Eastern newspapers for workers, offering them a dollar a day — double the going rate. By the fall of 1901, the standard-gauge Bradshaw Mountain Railroad was under construction. It had two branches. The shorter extended eight miles from Poland Junction to Murphy's mining interests at Poland. It was completed in seven months. The biggest delay was caused in January of 1902 when a railroad construction blast exposed a huge body of gold and copper ore. Half the work force forgot about railroading and became miners. Two carloads of workers were hurriedly imported from the East to replace the first crew.

The longer route, from Mayer through Cedar Canyon to Turkey Creek and then up the eastern face of the Bradshaws, took three years. The cost was three times the estimate, and the steep grade required five pairs of switchbacks, a tunnel, and several incredibly high trestles. But the tracks finally reached Crown King in 1904, and "Murphy's Impossible Railroad" was a reality.

During its existence, the Bradshaw Mountain Railroad transported about $1.1 million in gold and silver from the Pine Grove, Tiger, Big Bug, Turkey Creek, and Crown

King mining districts. Eventually the ore bodies played out and the mines closed. The tracks were taken up in 1927, leaving back-roads auto travelers a marvelous route to visit the ghost towns and mining camps of the eastern Bradshaws.

Humboldt was settled in the 1860s. This community in the Agua Fria Valley was originally called Val Verde, for a smelter of that name which processed the copper and lead of the Blue Bell and De Soto mines. At one point the Blue Bell, owned and operated by the Consolidated Arizona Smelting Company, shipped 11,000 tons of ore monthly. The commercial section of town was built on a ridge, with Main Street running down the center. Company houses and other buildings occupied the gulches on either side, while high-class houses were located on Nob Hill, near the smelter.

A post office opened in 1899 as Val Verde but was renamed Humboldt in 1905 to honor Baron Alexander von Humboldt (1769-1859), who had predicted more than a century earlier that "the riches of the world would be found" in the vicinity of the Bradshaw Mountains. As other mines were discovered in the area, more ore was sent to Humboldt. The expansion of smelting operations naturally meant prosperity for the town. The community eventually had a school, a telephone exchange, a bank, an ice house, a hospital, the Tisdale Hotel, Wingfield's Mercantile, the Humboldt Commercial Company,

saloons, and pool halls.

In the midst of the prosperity, however, two fires struck the community. The first, in 1909, burned down the Tisdale Hotel and the Humboldt Commercial Company. The second, a year later, destroyed 15 buildings in one of the gulches.

After World War I, the mines shut down and smelting ceased. The town was deserted by 1924. A 1926 article in the *Miami Silver Belt* warned, "Another lesson to be learned from the experience of Humboldt is that any community should strive earnestly and consistently to work itself out of a situation wherein its commercial and industrial existence is entirely dependent upon a single industry." That is much easier said than done. However, Humboldt was resurrected in 1934, when Fred Gibbs acquired the Iron King Mine, which produced more than $100 million in lead and zinc until its closure in 1968.

Today only one stack, some slag piles, and the brick walls of the smelters remain. In 1955 a stack built in 1899 was deemed a hazard, so school was recessed to let children watch the old stack topple. Several false-front buildings from the '20s and '30s remain on Main Street along with the Bank of Humboldt. The bank failed in the 1930s, and the building now serves as a church. A side street, once the old Black Canyon Highway, has a false-front store, vintage gas station, and a made-for-tourists "old" Western town.

Mayer is situated where, in 1882, Joe Mayer built a store that also had overnight accommodations for travelers. It was so successful that he added a stage station and saloon. Mayer's store was the handiest place around. Cattlemen would lodge there while laying out $3,000 or $4,000 for reprovisioning.

As mines opened at Stoddard, Copper Mountain, and Poland, the town expanded. It received a post office in 1884, and two years later Joe Mayer constructed the two-story Mayer Hotel. The Prescott and Eastern Railroad arrived in 1898, further solidifying the community's importance as a center of commerce.

Joe Mayer was a natural entrepreneur. A 1902 issue of the *Prescott Journal-Miner* reports that Mayer, in partnership with E.S. Rogers, planned to market toothpicks made from cactus thorns as "Indian Souvenir Toothpicks." The newspaper had received a sample lot and was duly impressed.

Today, Mayer, located along State Route 69 between Interstate 17 and Prescott, remains a viable town that treasures its past. Several historic buildings are sprinkled throughout the town.

East of Mayer's main business center is the 1903 White House Hotel (now a private residence). Its two-story brick construction with double porches makes it look somewhat like a Mississippi riverboat.

The most obvious landmark in Mayer is the lone smokestack, 120 feet high, of the Great Western Smelter. Built in 1916, it was planned as part of a complex that would raise the daily capacity of the smelter from 200 to 700 tons. Great Western shut down, however, before the rest of the new works could be completed, and the smokestack was never put into use.

Elsewhere, at 12780 Central (also known as Lower Main Street) is a 1908 building constructed with red brick manaufactured in Mayer. Once a saloon and dance hall, it now is occupied by a shop. Next door, lies a 1930 building that once was the town's post office, and across the street is the 1918 Mayer State Bank Building.

(Far Left) *Deep in the earth, a miner operates a drill in a mine near Humboldt. The town was all but deserted by 1924, but 10 years later it was resurrected when the Iron King Mine resumed production.*
SHARLOT HALL MUSEUM

(Left, Above) *The White House Hotel in Mayer, which could be mistaken for a Mississippi River stern-wheeler, was built in 1903. It is now a private residence.*
PHILIP VARNEY

(Left, Below) *This dredge, operating near Mayer, offered another means of extracting gold.*
SHARLOT HALL MUSEUM

And on Main Street, between 4th and 5th Streets, is the Red Brick Schoolhouse, built in 1913 and which still has the school's original bell. Details on historic buildings are available online at www.arizonahighway69chamber.org.

Cordes is 8 miles southeast of Mayer. John Henry Cordes came to New York from his native Germany in 1869. There he fell in love with Elise Schrimpfh, another German immigrant. In true Western tradition, Cordes left New York in 1875 to seek his fortune so that he could send for her. He went via the Isthmus of Panama to San Francisco, then down the coast to Los Angeles. In 1877 he embarked on another voyage, this time around the southern tip of Baja California and up the Colorado River to Yuma Crossing. He sent for Elise and married her in Phoenix in 1880.

In 1883, Cordes, his wife "Lizzie," and year-old son Charles moved north to Antelope Station, where for $769.43 he purchased a small adobe stage stop along the route of the California and Arizona Stage Company. When Cordes applied for a post office as Antelope Station, he was turned down because of possible confusion with another Antelope Station (later called Stanton, see p. 28). As an alternate, Cordes chose his family name and served as the first postmaster.

When mines opened in the area, the outpost became a supply depot and bank for the miners. It later became a stop for sheep drives en route to winter or summer ranges. Eventually Murphy's Impossible Railroad built a siding called Cordes Station, 3 miles to the west at Cedar Canyon.

Over the years at Cordes, Lizzie bore six more children. This hard-working family had some enjoyment. After the Bradshaw Mountain Railroad established Cordes Station, the Cordes family would celebrate the Fourth of July by picking up a 100-pound block of ice in a gunnysack dropped at the railroad siding. By the time they returned home the ice weighed only 75 pounds. Family members took turns working the hand-cranked freezer, relishing their once-a-year ice cream treat.

Cordes' eldest son, Charles, took over his father's business in 1908 after attending Los Angeles Business College. In 1909 he jacked up the roof of the old stage-station-turned-house to repair it. Finding the adobe walls in terrible shape, he built a new wood-frame house before lowering the roof into position. In 1914 he constructed a new store that contained a saloon and warehouse. Charles turned the business over to his eldest son, Henry, in 1938. The store caught fire in 1940, but nearby miners helped remove merchandise, so none was lost. Henry immediately rebuilt.

The Cordes post office closed in 1944, but the town lived on until the 1950s, when it was bypassed by the Black Canyon Freeway. A new stopping place, Cordes Junction, was established. The Cordes family got in on the ground floor there, too. In anticipation of the new route, three Cordes brothers filed homestead claims. A gas station and restaurant at the junction today were built by Henry Cordes.

Still standing at the original townsite is a combination gas station and store (now a private residence) that closed in 1973, the family home, and a barn constructed in 1912. The Cordes family continues to live at the site, a testament to the pioneer tradition of putting down roots, doing hard, enterprising work, and adapting to the changing times.

Bumble Bee is about 8 miles south of Cordes. Nearby Bumble Bee Creek received its name about 1863. One likely story says the appellation came from a U.S. Cavalry detachment led by a Colonel Powers, who had a tempo- rary outpost there and reported that Indians were "as thick as bumblebees." Another says that gold prospectors were attacked by a swarm along the creek as they searched for placer deposits.

For a short while, placer claims along Bumble Bee Creek paid well — at least if you were selling them. Many hopeful novices paid up to $150 for "blanket claims," so-called because they were no larger than a bed quilt.

A stage stop established near the creek was known as Snyder's Station, for local rancher W.W. Snyder. When the post office was granted in 1879, however, it was for Bumble Bee. Fortunately ranching was the mainstay of the valley, because local mines like the Hidden Treasure, Gloriana, Portuguese Bar, China Bar, and Dead Man contributed little to the economy. As a Bumble Bee citizen once eloquently wrote, "There were prospect holes all over the hills, though nothing ever amounted to much. But we had doors opening toward the stars."

The structures in present-day Bumble Bee were built

During the first decade of the 20th century, the town of Cleator in the Bradshaw Mountains was a busy amalgam of miners, railroad workers, and ranchers — a social center where everyone came to dance and drink on weekend nights. This old stone schoolhouse is a forlorn reminder of those days.
PHILIP VARNEY

in the late 1930s by Jeff Martin. The town was put up for sale in 1949, but it wasn't until Eastern magazine publisher Charles A. Penn purchased it in 1960 that the community made the wire services. Penn was touted as the only person in the United States at that time who owned an entire township. Ironically, only a few miles up the road lived Tom Cleator, who proved Penn's claim was erroneous. Penn planned to restore the town and create an authentic model-railroad museum. It never happened.

In Bumble Bee today the trading post is closed and posted against trespassing. Penn's home is occupied, and the WPA-built school has been turned into a residence. A series of row houses that were in poor repair in the 1980s has been admirably renovated.

Cleator is where the old route of Murphy's Impossible Railroad, having gone through Cedar Canyon, becomes today's dirt road to Crown King.

The road heading south from Cordes soon drops off the plateau, and one can clearly see a small cluster of

The Cleator store, the heart of the century-old ghost town, is closed, but the adjacent bar is open. PHILIP VARNEY

buildings along Turkey Creek as well as the dramatic eastern face of the Bradshaws. It is hard to imagine planning, much less completing, a railroad on that formidable terrain.

The Turkey Creek Mining District was a placer gold site established in 1864 as prospectors fanned out from Walker (see p. 22) to find the next bonanza. After a stage station was constructed two miles west of the creek in 1869, a post office was granted at Turkey Creek. But it lasted only five months.

The placer workings gave out quickly, but mines in the foothills took their place. By 1902 when Murphy's Impossible Railroad reached Turkey Station (also called Turkey Creek Station and Turkey Siding), several mines were ready customers for cheap ore transportation.

Leverett "Lev" Pierce Nellis had arrived a year before. In anticipation of the railroad, he had built a store and saloon and reopened the post office. Within a couple of years he owned most of the growing town.

James P. Cleator came to Turkey Creek soon afterward. Born on the Isle of Man in 1870, Cleator went to sea as a cabin boy at age 12. At 16 he signed on as an able seaman for a voyage to Spain. In 1889 he came to America and quit the sea. He would proudly recall that in San Francisco he shook the hand of President Benjamin Harrison. After making $10,000 on a California mining claim, he came to Arizona via Mexico in 1900.

Jimmie Cleator approached Lev Nellis in 1905 about buying into Nellis' business. Nellis agreed. The partnership worked so well that they expanded into ranching. In 1915 they amicably split the partnership, Nellis taking the cattle and $2,500 and Cleator getting the town. Ten years later, postmaster James P. Cleator had the post office renamed after himself.

Cleator was a lively place where ranchers, miners, and railroad workers converged. Mynne Cordes Jarman fondly remembered the Cordes girls riding to the store in Cleator for dances with local ranch hands and miners.

Cleator eventually declined in the late 1920s as mines closed. Jimmie Cleator, who had married in 1919 after almost 50 years of bachelorhood, then had a wife, two children, a shut-down mine, and a ghost town. He put Cleator up for sale in 1949 but had no takers. The post office closed in 1954. Jimmie Cleator died five years later, leaving the town to his son, Tom.

A WPA-built stone schoolhouse and about a dozen cabins still stand at Cleator. The original Cleator store is closed, but the adjacent saloon, site of those gala dances, is open from 10 A.M. to 8 P.M. Until his death, in 1996 at age 71, Tom Cleator hosted visitors there, telling stories of the Cleator clan that has been such an integral part of the surrounding country. Resting in the quiet, high desert on the east slope of the Bradshaw Mountains, a little more than an hour's drive from Phoenix, Cleator is a relaxing place to stop and seems like a thousand miles and a hundred years away from modern city life.

Traversing Murphy's Impossible Railroad is not impossible at all. The dirt road heading southwest from Cleator is the roadbed of the old Bradshaw Mountain Railroad. Evidence of this are backfilled dips, gentle curves, and deep cuts made in the rock, traits that are roadbed requirements for trains, not automobiles. About 2.5 miles out of Cleator the road passes the site of Middleton, where a .75-mile-long tramway once delivered ore to the railway from the De Soto Mine. Remnants of that tramway extend west up the mountain to the mine.

After climbing gently, the roadbed becomes a series of very steep switchbacks. Most motorists think a "switchback" is simply a hairpin turn. But to a railroader it's something very different. At a switchback, the train goes into a spur beyond the turn, a switch is thrown, and the train backs up to the next such switchback, where the process repeats itself, and the train goes forward once again. The railroad to Crown King had five

pairs of these switchbacks. The road today follows two of the pairs. Motorists should be sure to look at the cutaways the railroad made to allow the switches to be thrown. If the turn goes to the right, for example, look left to see where the train was positioned to climb the next part of the grade.

At places where trestles were used, the old roadbed clearly heads off into space (now blocked by earth and/or signs). Today's dirt road takes much tighter turns until rejoining the railroad bed. An interesting sidelight: When the tracks were taken up in 1927, Model T-era vehicles drove the trestles on boards strung along the towering structures at wheel width. There was little room for error in judgment. There was also very little drinking at weekly dances held in the schoolhouse at Crown King, as participants considered the treacherous midnight drive home.

Nearing its destination the dirt road detours around a now-collapsed tunnel, crosses a bridge, and enters a forested paradise. Welcome to Crown King.

Crown King is named after the Crowned King Mine, which was discovered in the early 1870s. The mine was supposed to be the biggest bonanza of the "Bradshaw

This is an engineer's view of the railroad approach to Crown King some 80 years ago when that Bradshaw Mountain town was a mining center with 500 buildings. In recent decades, Crown King has become a resort and summer-home community.
SHARLOT HALL MUSEUM

The Crown King restaurant and saloon is a nostalgic link with the Old West and well worth driving many miles to visit.
PHILIP VARNEY

Excitement." A Prescott paper made colossal exaggerations, describing "ore that runs $180,000 to the ton" and calling it "The Richest Strike in the History of Arizona!" Difficulties in recovering the gold, compounded with the tremendous cost ($21.50 per ton) to haul ore via pack train to Prescott, made the mine less of a bonanza than hoped. In the late 1880s, George P. Harrington came to the Crowned King and seemed to bring good luck with him. Several discoveries of gold considerably increased the mine's prospects. By 1888, the town's name was shortened to Crown King, and it featured 500 buildings and a post office — with George P. Harrington as postmaster.

By 1897 Crown King had electricity, one telephone, company stores, boardinghouses, saloons, and two Chinese restaurants. Even with the presence of the saloons, the town was known as a sedate place, as the mining companies did not tolerate unseemly behavior.

The arrival of Murphy's Impossible Railroad in 1904 solved the transportation troubles. Ironically, an ownership dispute and lawsuits had closed the mine, which up to that time had produced more than $1.5 million in gold. Harrington departed Crown King to oversee operations at the Oro Belle Mine, five miles to the southwest.

Although the railroad carried the wealth of area mines for another two decades, the best days of Crown King had already passed.

As the closest escape from Phoenix summer heat, Crown King has become a mecca of private cabins, rentals, and nearby camping spots. The center of activity is the Crown King General Store, which dates from the town's heyday more than a century ago. A second historic building is the saloon-restaurant, brought piece by piece on pack mules from Oro Belle about 1910. The upstairs had rooms to rent "for a few minutes," as one wag put it. Inside the saloon are some outstanding photographs of Crown King, Oro Belle, and the Prescott and Eastern Railroad.

Two other historic attractions remain. Immediately after turning into Crown King, a road to the right (north) parallels the road travelers come in on, but on the west side of the creek. It soon crosses a bridge and loops left, becoming Tower Mountain Road. That road, after .2 mile, passes the well-maintained Crown King School, which also serves as a library. Naturally, in the tradition of country schools, it is painted bright red. Another .7 of a mile up the road is the intersection of Tower Mountain Road and Torpedo Road. Follow Torpedo Road .2 mile, then take the right fork in .1 mile to the Crown King Cemetery, one of the most peaceful, scenic spots in the Bradshaws. You will recognize it by the distinctive, cross-topped wire fence.

Beyond Crown King

For the purist with a high-clearance vehicle, ghost town exploring doesn't have to stop at Crown King. The site of **Bradshaw City,** named for prospector William Bradshaw, is 1.9 miles west of Crown King along the Senator Highway toward Prescott. Today only a Forest Service sign marks the location, which is a popular camping place. A former road, which the forest service has allowed to deteriorate into what I would call an all-terrain vehicle trail, heads south (.2

Miners in the Bradshaw Mountain foothills of Yavapai County, circa 1890, used "dry rockers" to separate gold dust from sand and rock fragments. The device rocked the sand back and forth and the heavier gold particles lodged in corrugations, much the same as when placer miners sloshed it around in a pan.
SHARLOT HALL MUSEUM

mile before reaching Bradshaw City) and arrives in .5 of a mile at the trailhead to the Bradshaw City Cemetery, where slight evidence remains. The ghost of Oro Belle, 2.5 miles beyond the Bradshaw City Cemetery trailhead, features ruins of the mine and the Tiger Gold Company Store, as well as other debris.

In good weather, a high-clearance vehicle can make the often-rutty road beyond the Bradshaw City townsite sign (not the "road" to Oro Belle) into a loop drive by continuing north to Prescott on the Senator Highway via Palace Station and either Maxton or Walker. Check your gas gauge and allow several hours for this trip. Do not attempt the route during or after rains.

WHEN YOU GO: Humboldt is 17 miles east of Prescott on State Route 69. Mayer is 8 miles south of Humboldt on State 69. Cordes is nearly 8 miles southeast of Mayer on Antelope Creek Road, a dirt road leading from 69. (For a side trip, continue on the road to Bumble Bee, 8 miles south of Cordes.) On FR 259, Cleator is 7 miles southwest of Cordes, and Crown King is 13 miles more up the mountain. These sites can be reached with a passenger car during fair weather. Travel beyond Crown King, however, requires a high-clearance vehicle.

Walker and Palace Station

Walker began in the decades that followed the California gold rush of 1849. People went scurrying into unexplored hills all over the West. In 1863, Capt. Joseph Rutherford (occasionally listed as Reddeford) Walker, who served with Kit Carson, led a group of 33 adventurers from New Mexico to Tucson and up through the middle of the Arizona Territory. Menaced by Indians and sti-

fled by heat, they journeyed along the Hassayampa River into what would be named the Bradshaw Mountains and built a small fort near the present city of Prescott. The gold seekers discovered placer deposits along a creek called Ookilsipava. It was supposedly renamed Lynx Creek when one of the prospectors found a lynx beside the creek and, taking it for dead, lifted it — only to make the startling and painful discovery that it was still very much alive.

Because Lynx Creek not only had placer gold, but also primary deposits in the surrounding hills, the Walker party moved its settlement to the new find and named it in honor of their leader.

The community of Walker sustained mining activity into the 1940s. Weekend gold-panners still occasionally

that road, a small forest service sign marks the start of the trailhead. From there it's a five-minute walk.

Palace Station is one of several mining camps that once dotted the Bradshaw Mountains south of Prescott. It nestles comfortably beside the Senator Highway, the dirt road that leads to Crown King. Most sites have vanished, including Senator, Maxton, Venezia, Bueno, and Goodwin. However, one very interesting structure still stands.

Alfred B. Spence, his wife Matilda, and her father, R.J. Lambuth, came to the Arizona Territory in 1873. They settled in Groom Creek, where Spence opened a sawmill. Two years later they moved to Crook's Canyon, named for Indian fighter Gen. George Crook, where they built the cabin that is one of the oldest remaining pioneer buildings in the state. Spence chose the location because it was halfway between Prescott and the then-flourishing Peck Mine (which was about 7 miles north of Crown King).

By 1877 a branch line of the Prescott and Phoenix Stage was stopping at the cabin, known as Palace Station, en route to the Peck Mine. Passengers were fed by Mrs. Spence while the horses were watered. Although stage passengers did not spend the night, many other travelers did. The station also had a bar and served as a social center for miners working claims in the area. The Spences' daughter Elsie, born in 1882, recalled in a 1978 interview that she used to peek at the "fancy ladies" who arrived by stage to "visit" the miners once a month on payday.

Alfred Spence died in 1908 and is buried in the nearby cemetery, as are his father-in-law and perhaps a dozen other people. Automobiles and the telephone eventually made the stage line obsolete. Mrs. Spence sold the station in 1910.

Palace Station is now used by the Forest Service. Although it is not open to the public, visitors can explore its grounds and view the building's exterior. While many frontier buildings have been destroyed, modified beyond recognition, or moved to museum locations, Palace Station gives an authentic glimpse of the past.

WHEN YOU GO: Mount Vernon Street in Prescott becomes the Senator Highway. Palace Station is 16 miles south. A high-clearance vehicle is required. This is a trip to be made only in fair weather.

work the area's creeks. In its heyday Walker had 2,700 residents and featured the usual stores and saloons, along with a school, jail, and hospital. A post office opened in 1879, but by that time the peak of excitement had passed. It closed in 1940. Today, visitors to the area would never suspect that Walker was once the scene of feverish activity. The creek now is lined with summer cabins and year-round homes. Only a Forest Service sign marks the original townsite.

One important relic remains — a stone charcoal kiln standing silently among the pines. It was built about 1880 by Jake and Joe Carmichael to provide charcoal for Walker-area smelters. Outdoor barbecuers know that charcoal is preferable to wood because it burns longer and at a higher temperature. Charcoal is created by controlling the burning of wood. In this and similar kilns (see Cochran, p. 91), wood was stacked vertically through a ground-level entrance. The last wood was placed through a high rear opening reached by a short trestle. After lighting a fire in the center, the mouths of the kiln were sealed. A controlled amount of air entered through small holes around the sides. After several days of slow burning, the charcoal was removed and shipped to smelters.

The beautiful surrounding pines, incidentally, are relatively new growth. When this kiln was in operation, the entire forest had been stripped to supply it.

WHEN YOU GO: Walker is 12 miles southeast of Prescott on Walker Road, which intersects with State Route 69 east of Prescott. To reach the kiln, drive north .7 of a mile from the junction of Walker Road and Big Bug Mesa Road, where the Forest Service sign tells about Walker. A sign marks the turnoff west to the kiln on Charcoal Kiln Road. Among some large homes along

CHAPTER 2

Vulture Ghosts

Hollywood loves to dramatize the history of the West: The lonely prospector strikes a major vein only to have someone cheat him out of his fair share. Despondent, the poor man takes his own life. Or how about this: An unprincipled opportunist comes to a small town, gains the confidence of the citizens, and eventually takes over the community, only to be murdered by the brother of a woman he sullied.

Don't these sound like standard Western-movie fare? Ironically, these tales didn't spring from the minds of Hollywood screenwriters. They are true stories played out by real people in the once-thriving towns of Vulture and Stanton.

Vulture, one of the more extensive mining sites in the Old West, was closed to the public for many years, frustrating ghost town enthusiasts. At this writing, however, it is open for self-guided tours, with a nominal admission fee.

Stanton was off-limits until the late 1970s, when the Lost Dutchman Mining Association purchased the town

for its members' use. Although Stanton is private property, the association welcomes visitors. These two towns and the well-preserved buildings that remain are special points of interest in an area rich in lore and history.

The Vulture

Prospector Henry Wickenburg came to Arizona from Austria in 1862 and discovered a promising outcropping of gold quartz a year later. Further investigation proved him right — he had indeed discovered a rich deposit.

Two stories address his naming the claim the Vulture. One suggests he found the quartz while retrieving a vulture he shot. Since there is no great purpose to wasting ammunition on a buzzard (unless it sees you as a prospective meal), this probably is not an accurate accounting. A second, more plausible, version is that on the day Henry Wickenburg made his discovery, he saw several of the big birds circling the mountain now known as Vulture Peak. As one

(Above) *Residents of Vulture in the early 1860s.*
Desert Caballeros Western Museum
(Facing Page, Above) *A building that housed miners at Vulture still contains authentic relics of the period.*
(Facing Page, Below) *Vulture once had two schoolhouses.*
Both by Philip Varney

24

of Arizona's richest gold mines, the Vulture became an important supplier of bullion for the Union cause during the Civil War.

Henry Wickenburg was not a "hard rock" miner. Instead of doing the work, he contracted others to do the mining and milling, keeping a flat $15 per ton for himself. In 1866 Benjamin Phelps purchased an 80-percent interest in the mine, but, according to one account, never paid Wickenburg the total agreed-upon price. Wickenburg, who preferred other pursuits to begin with, left mining and tried the cattle business. His Wickenburg Ranch established the place-name for the town that bears his name. In the first six years of Phelps' mining operation, more than $2.5 million in gold was "officially" extracted. Unofficially, the total was believed to have been far higher: An estimated 20 percent to 40 percent of the ore is believed to have been "high-graded" (stolen) by the miners who worked there. One account says 18 of the high-graders were hanged.

James Seymour purchased the mine in 1878, despite popular sentiment that the veins had played out. Seymour's instincts were right. The Vulture came back to life with such vigor that Seymour added a stamp mill along the Hassayampa River, about 12 miles from the mine. He named the community that formed around the stamp mill after himself. Then, in 1880, the mill was dismantled, moved to the Vulture to furnish parts for a new mill, and the town of Seymour died.

The Vulture thrived well into the 1890s. The town featured a large stone assay office, miners' dormitories, houses for company officials, a mess hall, a school, a post office, and an 80-stamp mill. The post office closed in 1897, although production continued on a diminished scale through the 1920s. In fact, it was not until 1942, when President Roosevelt's Executive Order 208 banned mining of non-strategic material during World War II, that production ceased.

Henry Wickenburg, who was left behind during the Vulture's prosperous years, was not a successful rancher either. In 1905, elderly and penniless, he killed himself with a Colt revolver.

But Wickenburg's legacy remains. He donated to settlers a portion of his land where the town bearing his name now stands, and the strike that he made at Vulture had a tremendous impact on Arizona's development. Before his discovery, the area between Tucson and Prescott was virtually uninhabited by Anglos. When Vulture became the third-largest town in the Territory, the need for food for miners and feed for livestock increased dramatically. The solution lay in a community 60 miles to the southeast and the irrigated farmlands of

(Above) *The mess hall kitchen's mammoth cast-iron range still appears ready to satisfy a slew of hungry miners.*
(Left) *Ghost town buffs find the Vulture Mine a "must visit" because of its well-preserved structures, including the assay office where the gold ore was tested.*
BOTH BY PHILIP VARNEY
(Right) *Discovered by Henry Wickenburg in 1863, the Vulture Mine was still a rich gold producer in the mid-1890s when these workers were on the scene.*
ARIZONA HISTORICAL SOCIETY

the Salt River Valley. Phoenix began to grow.

Present-day Vulture features several buildings under roof, including a two-story assay office, a blacksmith shop, ball mill, power-house, bunkhouse, kitchen, mining officials' residences, and a schoolhouse. Almost every building features interesting items of antiquity, including a marvelous wooden ice box in the rear of the kitchen and an enormous 1904 German diesel engine in the power-house.

Almost lost amidst these impressive structures are the walls of Henry Wickenburg's tiny rock and adobe home. They stand mute in the shade of the "hanging tree" from which the 18 high-grading thieves are said to have swung.

WHEN YOU GO: Vulture is 3 miles west of Wickenburg on U.S. Route 60, then south 11 miles on Vulture Mine Road. For more information, contact the mine operator, (602) 859-2743.

The Ghosts of Rich Hill

In 1863, the same year Henry Wickenburg discovered the Vulture lode, Pauline Weaver, a famous Western explorer and scout, led a group organized by Abraham Harlow Peeples from Yuma into the central Arizona ter-

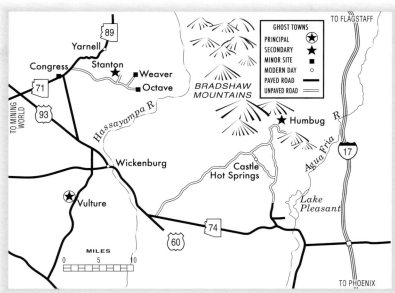

ritory. One reminder of that expedition is Peeples Valley, north of Yarnell. Peeples established a ranch there in 1865 before moving to Wickenburg five years later.

Another more dramatic legacy resulted from an earlier stop the expedition made. One evening the party killed three antelope and camped along a stream at the base of a rock-strewn hill. While some men looked for placer gold along the creek, a man named Alvaro climbed the hill and found a one-acre basin containing gold nuggets. The stream became Antelope Creek, the canyon on the east side of the mountain became Weaver Gulch, and the

hill that contained the mother lode was appropriately called Rich Hill. Three communities grew from that fortuitous strike.

Stanton, originally called Antelope Station, was a small community that developed along Antelope Creek. Most of the residents were miners, but some merchants settled there too, providing goods and services. The stage station owner was an Englishman named William Partridge. The general store was owned by G.H. "Yaqui" Wilson. Pigs belonging to Wilson broke into Partridge's property, beginning an enmity that was to serve a newcomer well.

Charles P. Stanton came to Antelope Station in the early 1870s, having left the post of assayer at the Vulture Mine. He conceived a plan to use the Partridge-Wilson feud to eliminate both men, which he believed would leave the two principal commercial enterprises of Antelope Station in his hands. He told Partridge, "The owner of the pigs is out to get you," a statement that was patently false. Partridge, however, believed the threat and shot Wilson on sight. Partridge was arrested, tried, convicted, and sentenced to prison in Yuma, where he claimed to be haunted by Wilson's ghost.

However, things didn't immediately go as Stanton had planned. Wilson had a silent partner named Timmerman. And the incarcerated Partridge had creditors, who sold his stage station to Barney Martin. Undeterred, Stanton hired a group of desperadoes led by a man named Francisco Vega to dispose of Timmerman. This done, in 1875 the town was renamed Stanton, with Charles P. Stanton as postmaster. Besides Stanton, the only remaining person of power was Barney Martin. In July of 1886 the remains of Martin, his wife, and children were found in a charred wagon not far from town.

Charles Stanton brutally achieved the control he sought. But not for long. In November of the same year, a young member of the Vega gang, Cristero Lucero, shot Stanton to death because Stanton had insulted his sister. As he fled town, Lucero met another Stanton adversary, Tom Pierson. When Lucero told him what he had done, Pierson is said to have replied, "You don't have to pull out. If you stick around, you'll get a reward."

Within four years, Stanton, the town, was almost as

dead as Stanton, the man. The post office closed in 1890 as mines played out, then reopened in 1894 along with the mines. About 200 people lived in the community, which featured a new store, a boardinghouse, homes, and a five-stamp mill. The post office closed for good in 1905.

For many years Stanton was closed to the public, which probably accounts for its restorable state. Since purchasing the site in 1978, the Lost Dutchman Mining Association has improved roofing, shored walls, and, happily, allowed the public to visit. Only three buildings stand at Stanton today, but they are excellent reminders of the Old West.

One is Charles Stanton's old stage stop and store, in which he was murdered by Cristero Lucero. Another building, the most substantial structure on the site, was a saloon and now serves as a recreation hall. At the north end of the interior one can see where a shelf once was attached to the wall. It is not widely known, thanks to Western movies, that most saloons in the Old West did not have tables and chairs. Men stood around the periphery of the room, facing the center, their drinks positioned behind them on a narrow sill. This allowed imbibers to keep an eye on each other and anyone who came through the door. In a town with the likes of Charles Stanton, Fernando Vega, and Cristero Lucero, the arrangement had definite advantages.

The weathered Hotel Stanton is the other outstanding building at the townsite. Originally Partridge's stage station, the hotel features a main lobby and a series of rooms stretching down a boardwalk, each with its own front and back doors, another prudent architectural consideration for a town with a treacherous past.

(Below, Left) *The town of Stanton, as it appeared when this photo was taken in the late 1940s, had a violent history marked by murder plots and mayhem.*
JOSEF MUENCH
(Below) *Originally a stage station, the Hotel Stanton still stands more than a century after its construction. Stanton's three surviving buildings are open to the public and are well worth a visit.*
PHILIP VARNEY

Weaver gave new meaning to the word "dangerous" and made the town of Stanton look tame by comparison. Located on the eastern side of Rich Hill, along Weaver Creek, the town was first populated by miners working placer claims on Rich Hill. Eventually, as placer claims played out, Weaver became a refuge for thugs and cutthroats, some of whom were hired by Charles Stanton during his violent rise to power. After the 1898 murder of William Segna, the owner of a combination saloon-general store, a newspaper article called for the complete eradication of Weaver because of its unsavory

inhabitants. The town's few remaining law-abiding citizens left soon after Segna's murder, many relocating to the nearby town of Octave.

Weaver today offers several items of interest, including a rock corral; a cemetery of unmarked graves; the old rock walls of the two-room post office; and, up on a rise to the east, a small stone cool-house once used to store foodstuffs.

Octave has the most extensive mining remnants of the Rich Hill area. It features the concrete foundations of a mill, tailings, and three ramshackle buildings near a water tank. Mining continued at Octave until 1942, when Executive Order 208 went into effect and closed non-strategic mines.

Eight partners formed the Octave Gold Mining Company in 1863 to work claims south of the fabulously successful Rich Hill. However, Octave didn't become a mine or town of significance until the late 1890s. The post office established at Weaver in 1899 was transferred to Octave a year later as Weaver's population declined. Eventually, Octave had a stage stop, school, mercantile, and grocery store. One longtime resident of nearby Congress remembers that in the late 1930s Octave's big dances were the place to be on Friday nights.

WHEN YOU GO: Yavapai County Road 109, a dirt road suitable for passenger cars under normal conditions, heads east from State Route 89 almost 2 miles north of

(Above) Resourceful Weaver residents had no refrigerators, so they kept food in this stone cool-house.
(Right) So many thugs and murderers hung out at Weaver that some people wanted to wipe out the town completely. But there were enough stable residents to rate this two-room post office.
BOTH BY PHILIP VARNEY
(Facing Page) At the turn of the century, this wagon delivered mail to folks in Congress and Congress Junction.
DESERT CABALLEROS WESTERN MUSEUM

Congress. First comes Stanton, just over 6 miles east of State 89. To reach Weaver, continue east past Stanton for 1.8 miles (you will cross usually dry Weaver Creek) and take the rough road heading north for about a mile to the site. The remains of Octave are .3 of a mile east of the Weaver turnoff. A high-clearance vehicle is required to reach the two latter sites.

Additional Sites

Congress is an excellent example of just how much can disappear into the Arizona desert. The community was actually two separate places. "Mill Town," closer to the mine, featured the mill, company offices, a hospital, and residences. "Lower Town," located farther south, boasted the commercial district, including restaurants, the usual stores and saloons, two churches, and a school. Virtually nothing but debris remains at either site except for lasting testaments to man's presence: two cemeteries.

Congress sprang into existence after Dennis May's 1884 discovery of gold ore. The mine was sold in 1887 and then again in 1894, when the boom period began. The cost of transporting ore to market, the major shortcoming of many Arizona mines, was easily solved at Congress. By 1893 the Santa Fe, Prescott & Phoenix Railway passed within 3 miles of the mine. The station, known as Congress Junction, gave life to a small community that featured its own post office. In 1899, the Congress Consolidated Railroad was completed between the mine and Congress Junction.

The mining town prospered into the mid-1930s. The post office at Congress closed in August of 1938 and its name was transferred to the post office at Congress Junction on November 1st of that year. For all intents and purposes, the railroad community had become the only Congress and is so to this day.

The former Congress Junction has the only buildings for the ghost town enthusiast. The old Congress Hotel, a vacant residence, and two false-front buildings stand along the highway. The original school, across the railroad tracks to the west, now serves as the Congress Community Center.

The two cemeteries are reached, appropriately, via Ghost Town Road, which heads north of State Route 71 west of the railroad tracks. Follow the road for almost 2 miles. Signs direct you first to the Congress Cemetery and then to the Pioneer Cemetery.

The flagpole of the Congress Cemetery is easy to spot. Among several interesting grave markers is that of Oscar McIlroy, who was born in Center Point, Texas, in 1880, and buried at Congress in 1903. The inscription reads: "Sleep on dear boy, now take thy rest. God called thee home, he thought it best."

The Pioneer Cemetery is .6 of a mile farther down the road, which eventually loops back to Ghost Town Road.

Text continued on page 34

(Above) *The Congress Mine, 16 miles northwest of Wickenburg, dates back to 1884 when Dennis May discovered gold. By 1901 the mine and town were so famous that President William McKinley stopped here during his inspection trip to determine whether the Arizona Territory was ready for statehood.*
ARIZONA HISTORICAL SOCIETY

(Right) *The old Congress Hotel, now a vacant residence, another empty building fragile with old age, and this weather-beaten warehouse are all that remains of the buildings from Congress Junction's glory days.*
PHILIP VARNEY

(Left) *Lunch buckets or lunch pails such as these were used in the early days of mining in the Southwest. Considering how many thousands there must have been, they are an extremely rare collector's item today.*
ARIZONA HISTORICAL SOCIETY

(Left) *A worker in the Congress Mine (c. 1900) poses with a mine car used to transport ore to the surface. This drift, or horizontal tunnel, is 1700 feet underground. Note the shiny lunch buckets.*
SHARLOT HALL MUSEUM

(Below) *This grave in the Pioneer Cemetery at Congress is one of many in the area's two cemeteries that interest history lovers.*
PHILIP VARNEY

Continued from page 31

(Segments of this route require a high-clearance vehicle.) To prevent further vandalism, graves are protected by a locked gate. When I last visited, the sky was overcast and somber, a perfect setting for the mood of this place. Many of the tombstones tell of promises, dreams, and lives unfulfilled. At least eight infant graves grace the site. Eloicita Mouelthrop died in 1898 at the age of one month and 10 days. Joseph Villetti was just beginning his third year of life when he died in 1897. The marker says his death was "Regretted by his beloved parents." His epitaph: "Gone to be an angel."

WHEN YOU GO: Congress is 16 miles north of Wickenburg at the junction of state routes 71 and 89.

The Gold Leaf Mine (Robson's Mining World), is one of the West's most interesting and least commercial private museums. While not a ghost town and never a traditional mining camp, this town has been created with an eye for detail that makes touring it a delight. Jeri Robson and her late husband Charles collected outstanding specimens of mining equipment and other antiques and placed them within easy public inspection.

A printing shop is filled with typesetting equipment, a barbershop displays tonsorial and surgical relics, and a general store features a display of never-worn shoes with their original boxes. There is much more, of course. The Robsons' museum emphasizes authenticity and history. It's easy to devote an hour or two to touring the town. A modest admission is charged. The town is open for special events only. Call ahead first for information before visiting.

The mining museum and frontier town are located on the site of the Gold Leaf Mine, which began operations some time before World War I. Around 1930 it became the Nella Meda, named for two sisters. Seven original buildings remain on the site: four miners' shacks, the superintendent's quarters, a cookhouse, and a blacksmith's shop. At the mine itself are a water tank, a partial headframe, mill foundations, bins, and a fenced-off shaft.

WHEN YOU GO: Robson's Mining World is 25 miles west of Wickenburg via U.S. Route 60, then 4 miles north on State Route 71 and follow the signs west on a dirt road; or go 20 miles southwest from Congress on State 71 and follow the signs. (928) 415-0983.

Humbug is perhaps the most pristine example of a historic Arizona mining camp, but its future is undecided.

(Above) *Francis de Lacey Hyde is shown at his Humbug Mine retreat with his daughter, Carolyn ("Tuffet"), in about 1940. An unidentified guest rides between them.*
RUTH GAISFORD COLLECTION
(Right) *Hyde's Humbug Mine assay office still stands.*
(Facing Page, Above) *Robson's Mining World, 26 miles west of Wickenburg, is a private Western museum on the site of the Gold Leaf Mine, which began operations before World War I. Seven original buildings remain.*
BOTH BY PHILIP VARNEY

Its owners are divided over whether to restore Humbug and open it to visitors or to reopen the long-defunct mine and explore it for new deposits while keeping the property closed to the public.

The Bradshaw excitement of the early 1860s (see Walker, pages 22-23) caused prospectors to canvass the area in search of new strikes. One creek in the southern Bradshaws was talked about as a place of great promise. It proved to be a dud and was called a "humbug," a name that stuck. In the 1870s, however, solid placer deposits were discovered at Humbug and nearby Columbia. By 1884 Humbug had a mill and associated buildings. A post office opened 10 years later at Columbia to serve both communities.

Because of the area's inaccessibility, mining operations were minimal until 1932, when Humbug Gold Mines, Inc., acquired the claims. The camp became home for about 100 people. The company had its own mill but shipped its concentrate for smelting to Miami, Arizona, and El Paso, Texas. The owner of Humbug Gold Mines was Francis "Frank" de Lacey Hyde, a New York stockbroker who moved to Tucson in 1932.

For Frank Hyde, Humbug was not only a gold (and later a tungsten) venture. It was the ultimate Western retreat. He built a second home there and would bring his wife, Elizabeth, and infant daughter, Carolyn, known as "Tuffet," up to the mine for extended stays. Tuffet became an accomplished horsewoman. An article in *The Christian Science Monitor* in April of 1944, when Tuffet was nearing her 14th birthday, tells of Hyde and his daughter taking rides at night to search for tungsten in scheelite with "mineral lamps" that utilized ultraviolet rays. On one such trip it began to rain heavily, so they sought refuge in an old mine shaft where a miner was making his home. The miner bragged of all the shaft's comforts, including carbide lamps and a radio. He also said he

hadn't seen so much as one scorpion or rattlesnake. Hyde turned on his blue light, scanned the tunnel, and four scorpions lit up the dark. Who knows if the miner ever got another good night's sleep in his homey paradise.

Mining attempts at Humbug ceased during World War II. In 1947, Tuffet, then a student at the University of Arizona, brought classmate Ruth Gaisford to Humbug. It was the first of many such escapes they took to the beauty and tranquility of the Bradshaws. Frank Hyde, by then divorced, visited Humbug for the last time in 1956 and died in Tucson in 1973 at the age of 75. Tuffet died in 1989 and left her one-third interest in Humbug to her lifelong friend Ruth Gaisford. For her, as it was for Frank and Tuffet Hyde, the town was not a mine, but a priceless retreat that must be preserved. Ruth, however, died in 1999.

At Humbug six buildings remain under roof: the Hydes' main house, a three-apartment guesthouse, the foreman's residence, an assay office, the kitchen-dining building, and a stable with a corral. Humbug displays extensive uses of stone. Some uses are functional, like the corral; others are decorative, like the elaborate patio and garden walls in front of the Hyde home. The ruins of several other residences dot both sides of the creek.

WHEN YOU GO: Humbug is north of Lake Pleasant and west of Interstate 17 on a four-wheel-drive road leading from the Lake Pleasant Road. A gate blocks the private road before the town comes into view.

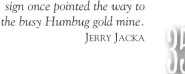

This weather-beaten sign once pointed the way to the busy Humbug gold mine.
JERRY JACKA

CHAPTER 3

Mohave Ghosts

To explore the Kingman area, 180 miles northwest of Phoenix, is to discover often unnoticed treasures. It is a delightful region with expansive Mohave Desert scenery, historic buildings, and interesting ghost towns. Yet most travelers hurry by, stopping just long enough to gas up and grab some fast food. They're on their way to Laughlin or Las Vegas, not realizing several "jackpots" lie much closer than that.

Kingman is situated along one of Arizona's most famous trails, known by several names over the years. The area was first explored for the United States government by Lt. Lorenzo Sitgreaves, whose party traversed northern Arizona along the 35th parallel in 1851.

The first actual trail was Beale's Wagon Road, established in 1857. Edward F. Beale, a Navy lieutenant, was given the assignment of plotting a wagon road to California. It was to follow the 35th parallel as closely as practicable. In addition to the standard army mules and wagons, Beale's expedition experimented with the use of camels, which he extolled as "noble brutes." Beale chose a white dromedary named

"Said" (Sah-eed) as his personal mount. Other wranglers on the trip had less favorable names for the camels, saying they frightened the horses and gave off a very unpleasant odor.

Westward development slowed during the next 25 years, first because of the Civil War and then because of countless Indian wars. The next "trail" was the Atlantic and Pacific Railroad (later the Atchison, Topeka, and Santa Fe). It was completed across Arizona in 1883. The locating engineer for the railroad was Lewis Kingman, who named the rail stop after himself. While completion of the railroad made Beale's wagon road obsolete, it also dramatically increased settlement throughout the area.

In 1937 Beale's road was transformed into a fully paved highway that became legendary U.S. Route 66, "The Main Street of America." Towns like Kingman and Oatman were more than railroad or mining enclaves. They were key supply stops during the great western movement that occurred during and after the Depression era, places where John Steinbeck's Joad family would

(Above) *Kingman began to dominate affairs in Mohave County after the arrival of the Atlantic and Pacific Railroad in 1883. This photo, c. 1905, shows travelers at Kingman's Harvey House restaurant.*
MOHAVE COUNTY HISTORICAL SOCIETY
(Facing Page) *Oatman folks are fiercely independent but must depend, in part, on tourist spending in such antique shops as the Glory Hole.*
PHILIP VARNEY

37

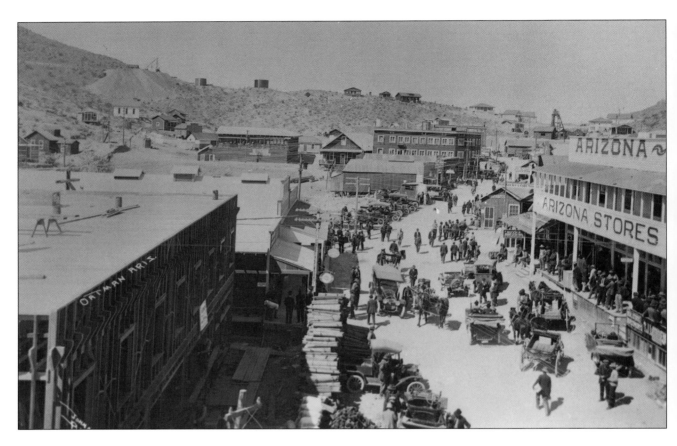

have scrounged together sufficient cash for gas and groceries. Route 66, of course, was replaced by Interstate 40. As a result, it is now possible, as newsman Charles Kuralt once commented, to go from coast to coast without seeing a thing.

Nevertheless, history buffs will find in Kingman alone several architecturally varied buildings. The stately Mohave County Courthouse, constructed in 1914, dominates the town square. Adjacent to it, in stark contrast, is a gloomy, dank jail that was built five years earlier. Former judge Clyde McCune once wryly remarked that, because of this jail, "We have very little recidivism." Nearby are the 1904 Elks Lodge, made of locally quarried stone, and the 1896 "Little Red Schoolhouse," now used by the city magistrate. Visitors can get a more complete picture of Kingman by touring the Mohave County Museum of History and Arts. Here an expansive exhibit is devoted to Kingman's own Andy Devine, the gravel-voiced actor who immortalized "Jingles," Wild Bill Hickok's television sidekick, with the plaintive cry, "Hey, Wild Bill, wait for me!"

Oatman and Goldroad

Oatman residents have one thing in common with residents of Arizona's other mining camps: feisty independence. They eschew the modern American rush to own the latest doohickey. In Oatman, that attitude is evident in spades.

Once a metropolis of some 10,000 people, Oatman was reduced in the 1950s to a population of about 60 after it was bypassed by the rerouted U.S. 66. Now the number is up to a few hundred, with many residents making a living selling items to tourists. They are a hardy bunch who look upon visitors with a bit of a defiant eye, knowing their dollars are necessary for their livelihood, but wishing they weren't. Frankly, I like their spirit.

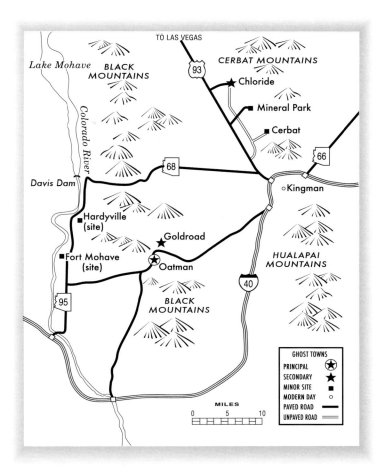

(Left, Above) *No Arizona mining town was busier or more optimistic than Oatman in 1916, when automobiles began outnumbering horses on Main Street.*
Mohave County Historical Society
(Left) *While the mines have closed down, Oatman still thrives as a Route 66 destination for tourists. Clark Gable and Carole Lombard honeymooned at the Oatman Hotel along Main Street.*
Philip Varney

When you take a drive up the road to Rockhound Hill, which redefines the term "paved," people may look at you as if to say, "Boy, are *you* lost!" But it is on back roads like this that you discover an Oatman different from the touristy main street.

That spirit of independence is not new to Oatman. Just after the turn of the century, miner Henry Ewing lost his eyesight while working his Nixon claim. Ignoring the pleas of friends concerned for his safety, Ewing continued his one-man operation by using guide wires as he dug, drilled, blasted, and timbered his mine. Along the way he survived a fall from a ladder and an encounter with an unfriendly rattlesnake. Foolhardy? Perhaps. Courageous? Absolutely.

Towering above the town of Oatman is a monolith known as Elephant's Tooth, a huge quartz outcropping that served as a signpost to prospectors, saying "look for gold right here." The original name of the town was Vivian, for the Vivian Mine discovered in 1902 by a mixed-blood Mojave named Ben Taddock (or Paddock, depending upon the source), who supposedly found gold glittering along a trail. Taddock sold his claim a year later to a judge and a colonel, who in turn sold it in 1905 to

the Vivian Mining Company, which fully developed the claim. By 1907, more than $3 million in gold had been extracted from the mine.

Vivian experienced a second boom in 1908 with the discovery of the Tom Reed Gold Mine. That year the town was renamed Oatman, a change the post office made official a year later. The new name honored Olive Oatman, a white girl who lived in captivity with a local Mojave Indian family for five years. Her safe return made the Oatman family's story famous throughout the West.

It began back in 1851 when Royce Oatman, his wife and seven children, en route to California, were attacked by a group of renegade Apaches or Yavapais about 25 miles west of present-day Gila Bend. They were all killed, except for sisters Olive, 13 or 14, and Mary Ann, 7 years old, who were abducted, and 16- or 17-year-old Lorenzo, who was thrown over a mesa edge and left for dead. Somehow, despite grievous wounds, Lorenzo lived and made his way back to safety.

After hearing persistent stories of a white girl living with the Indians along the Colorado River, Lorenzo, by then in his 20s, was in California trying to organize a search party when he heard of his sister's safe return to Fort Yuma. Although sickly Mary Ann had died in captivity during a time of drought, Olive was found among the peaceful Mojave, who had bought her from the renegades. She had married, apparently, as her traditional

Mojave facial tattoos indicated. But when another Indian came to the village asking for her and had horses and other items to trade, she was released and walked 200 miles to Yuma where she was soon met by her brother. After their reunion, Olive lived in Oregon and California for a short time. She married John B. Fairchild in 1865 and died in 1903 in Sherman, Texas.

John Oatman, reportedly Olive's Mojave son, lived in the Vivian area. Years after his mother died, he may have influenced the town's 1908 name change from Vivian to Oatman.

Following the Tom Reed gold vein discovery, another big strike occurred in 1913 when the United Eastern mine was opened. It was then that Oatman's population exploded to 10,000. The activity caused Wesley M. Barr to exclaim in *The Oatman Miner* in 1915, "... the automobile climbs the last grade and suddenly stops in the center of the most talked-of mining camp in America. Everywhere is activity. Everywhere is confidence and determination. The visitor mingles with the throngs in

(Left) *When the United Eastern Mine began operation in 1913, Oatman's population soared to 10,000. It was one of the area's "Big Three" mines, along with the Tom Reed and Goldroad.*
MOHAVE COUNTY HISTORICAL SOCIETY
(Left, Below) *The town of Vivian was renamed Oatman in 1908 in honor of Olive Oatman, a girl who was held captive by Mojave Indians near here in the 1850s.*
ARIZONA STATE LIBRARY, ARCHIVES AND PUBLIC RECORDS
(Right) *Goldroad, born from an 1899 gold strike, was a burgeoning town until the ore ran out about 1907.*
MOHAVE COUNTY HISTORICAL SOCIETY
(Below) *Only a few skeletons of buildings remain at Goldroad today.*
PHILIP VARNEY

the street, and above all he notes the absolute certainty on every face that Oatman has arrived, has removed its hat and is going to stay."

That "confidence and determination" continued well into the 1930s, when the Tom Reed finally shut down after bringing in more than $13 million in gold. With the closure of mines, the town found a less glamorous life as the last major stop along U.S. Route 66 before entering California and having to cross the seemingly endless Mohave Desert.

Main Street in Oatman features several buildings worth exploring, beginning with the Lee Lumber Company and the old movie theater, now souvenir shops. The Oatman Hotel, listed on the National Register of Historic Places, is Mohave County's only two-story adobe building and stands in the center of town. It features a bar and museum. Clark Gable and Carole Lombard honeymooned here after their wedding in Kingman. You can peek in on their room. A two-story

wooden false-front building at the far end of the street has been a drugstore during the Depression; the "Gold City Hotel," the role it played in the Oscar-winning movie *How the West Was Won;* and now, the Glory Hole, an antique shop (see photo on Page 37).

Humans aren't the only independent residents of Oatman. Wild burros, descendants of those let loose by miners, drop into town daily to cadge food from tourists. Try not to encourage them onto the boardwalks. As a shop owner said, burros leave more than footprints.

Goldroad stands in a canyon not far from Sitgreaves Pass on the way to Oatman along old U.S. Route 66. Lt. Edward Beale crossed this pass in October of 1857. Five months later Lt. Joseph Christmas Ives traversed the same pass, naming it for Lt. Lorenzo Sitgreaves, leader of the first expedition through the area. From here one has a sweeping view west to the expanding gambling mecca of Laughlin, Nevada, and southwest to California. Almost immediately upon descending the pass, one enters the mile-long ruins of Goldroad.

John Moss discovered traces of gold in the area in the early 1860s, but when silver ore was found in abundance in the Cerbat range, the modest Moss diggings were abandoned. About 1899 Jose Jerez, grubstaked to $12.50 by store owner Henry Lovin of Kingman, found a rich ledge of gold-bearing quartz. They sold their claim in 1901 for $50,000; within five years the same claim was worth 40 times that amount. Lovin used his money to open a mercantile, a successful freighting company, and the Goldroad Club. One of the regular customers at the club was Jose Jerez, who drank away most of his money

41

and ended his life by swallowing Rat-Be-Gone poison.

As it turned out, the community of Goldroad was short-lived. By 1907 the veins gave out and the mines closed. The site was razed in 1949 to save taxes.

Many travelers heading from Kingman to Oatman overlook Goldroad because the ruins blend in so well with the surrounding terrain. But for those who pull off the winding road to pause and look carefully, evidence is everywhere: rock retaining walls, roofless buildings, deteriorating adobe walls, concrete tanks, hoppers,

(Above) Rock-drilling competitions provided excitement at Goldroad in 1917. MOHAVE COUNTY HISTORICAL SOCIETY

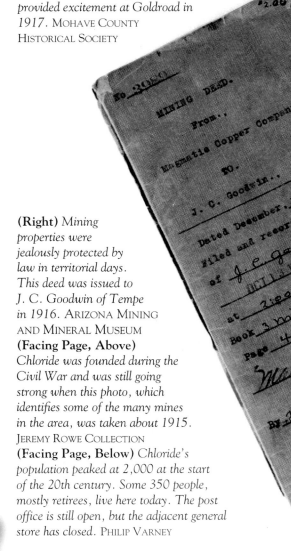

(Right) Mining properties were jealously protected by law in territorial days. This deed was issued to J. C. Goodwin of Tempe in 1916. ARIZONA MINING AND MINERAL MUSEUM
(Facing Page, Above) *Chloride was founded during the Civil War and was still going strong when this photo, which identifies some of the many mines in the area, was taken about 1915.* JEREMY ROWE COLLECTION
(Facing Page, Below) *Chloride's population peaked at 2,000 at the start of the 20th century. Some 350 people, mostly retirees, live here today. The post office is still open, but the adjacent general store has closed.* PHILIP VARNEY

and cement steps to nowhere. The Gold Road Mine, the same one discovered by Jose Jerez, is open for one-hour tours.

WHEN YOU GO: Oatman is 28 miles southwest of Kingman. Take Exit 44 from I-40. Goldroad is 3 miles before Oatman on the same road.

Chloride, Mineral Park, and Cerbat

Chloride was one of the earliest mining camps in the Arizona Territory. Named for silver chloride ore, the town grew from the Silver Hill strike of the 1860s. Reaching the isolated Silver Hill mines required taking a river steamboat 300 miles upstream from Yuma to Hardyville (now underwater near Bullhead City), and then crossing 38 miles of unforgiving desert.

It could be dangerous territory. In 1863, Hualapai Indians commandeered some miners' guns, shooting one and killing two more by throwing rocks down their mine shaft.

Undaunted by word of these occupational hazards, fortune seekers continued to come. Chloride became a full-fledged town in 1864 and received its post office nine years later. By 1900, the town had a population of 2,000. Its two major mines, the Tennessee and the Schuylkill, produced gold, silver, lead, and zinc on a major scale into the late 1940s. When the mines closed, the population declined, but the post office remained. Chloride has since seen a modest influx of people, primarily retirees, raising its population to about 350.

The town's main street features the post office and well-preserved false-front general store, which was built during 1928. North of the main street stand two original buildings, the jail (west of Second Street on Merrimac Street) and the old train depot (east of Second on Schuylkill Street). The town features several shops selling antiques and curios to tourists. The Tennessee and Schuylkill mines are east of town.

The cemetery, southwest of town on Patterson Lane, has an interesting older section. A monument there,

43

inscribed with a double heart, presents a riddle that will never be solved. Side by side lie the graves of young Jimmy and Howard Smith, born in 1928 and 1930. Both died on the same day, April 17, 1938.

Mineral Park, founded in 1871, was so named because of the rich cache of minerals in a parklike, juniper-filled basin at the foot of Ithaca Peak. It became the county seat in 1873, taking the title from nearby Cerbat. By the early 1880s Mineral Park not only featured paying mines but also served as a supply point for distant mines and a growing number of cattle ranches. It had all the usual mining camp ingredients: assay offices, a five-stamp mill, saloons, stores, and a post office. But it also had the trap-

pings of a sophisticated town: restaurants, a hotel, doctors and lawyers, two stagecoach stations, and a weekly newspaper, *The Mohave County Miner.* One reason prosperity shone so brightly was the completion in 1883 of the Atlantic and Pacific Railroad just 20 miles to the south, which cut the cost of transporting ore and supplies.

That same railroad, however, brought civic embarrassment to Mineral Park. The rail-stop town of Kingman grew so much faster than Mineral Park that by 1887 it had enough residents to claim the county seat. Despite a conclusive county-wide vote on the matter, Mineral Park officials refused to give up the county records. Outraged Kingman citizens subsequently raided Mineral Park, made off with the documents and, quite literally, took

the county seat.

Losing the county seat was a sign of things to come. The mines began closing after 1887. Some were reopened briefly in 1906, but the town was moribund. Its post office was closed in 1912.

Mineral Park has all but vanished. An open-pit mine, currently owned by Mercator Mineral Park and subleased to Mineral Park Decorative Rock, has caused once-prominent Ithaca Peak to disappear completely. Across the gulch, north of the mine, are scant remnants of earlier days. There, two miners' shacks, one adobe, another wood, decay on the hillside. The headframe of the Keystone Mine is farther up the hill.

The best reminder of Mineral Park is its small cemetery, one of the best-preserved in Arizona. Although it is within mine property, you can arrange to visit it by contacting Mercator Mineral Park Mine in advance. (928) 565-2226, ext. 231.

Cerbat was settled in the early 1860s not long after Chloride. A sister community to Mineral Park, it was the county seat for just two years. The town was named for the mountain range in which all three of these towns lie. Cerbat is an Indian word for bighorn sheep that once were common here.

Sustained by the Golden Gem, Esmeralda, and Vanderbilt mines, the community received its post office in December of 1872. The Golden Gem mill and headframe still stand, along with scattered debris, and a collapsed wooden residence. Be wary of a deep, uncovered shaft not far from the base of the mill.

WHEN YOU GO: Chloride is on a paved road about 20 miles northwest of Kingman off U.S. 93. The signed turnoff is about 14.5 miles past the junction of U.S. 93 and State Route 68. Chloride is 4 miles east of U.S. 93.

Two routes exist between Chloride and Mineral Park. You can return to U.S. 93, drive about 5 miles south, and turn east on Mineral Park Road. Mineral Park is 5 miles east of U.S. 93 on that road. A shorter route takes Chloride's Second Street south for 5.3 miles. It becomes a dirt road that is normally quite good (do not attempt this in rainy weather). Turn east on paved Mineral Park Road and head to the townsite, 3.4 miles away. To reach Cerbat from Mineral Park, return to the same intersection on Mineral Park Road (the north-south road is here called Old Boulder Dam Highway). Turn south and proceed for 3.1 miles, at which point the main road continues southwest. A more secondary road heads toward the Cerbat Mountains. Follow that road for 2.3 miles. The final .75 of a mile up the canyon requires a high-clearance vehicle or a willingness to walk.

Lamps like this, fueled with lard oil, were carried by miners or attached to ore wagons when a hard day's work extended into night.
JOHN DREW

CHAPTER 4

Ghosts of the Rivers

The Colorado River, an important source of water for both Arizona and Southern California, was once crucial for another reason: transportation. From 1852 until the arrival of the railroad in 1877, Colorado River paddle wheelers provided the cheapest, most reliable way to bring supplies to the Arizona Territory.

Martha Summerhayes, the new young wife of Army Lt. Jack Summerhayes, accompanied her husband to Arizona in 1870. Lieutenant Summerhayes was a supply officer in the Eighth Army, which Gen. George Crook planned to employ in the campaign against the Apaches. Martha's first impressions of the region are told in *Vanished Arizona*, a compelling account of frontier life:

. . . We came to anchor a mile or so off Port Isabel, at the mouth of the Colorado River . . . . And there we lay for three days before the sea was calm enough for the transfer of troops and baggage to the lighters.

This was excessively disagreeable. The wind was like a breath from a furnace; it seemed as though the days would never end . . . . On the fourth day . . . we boarded the river steamboat Cocopah, towing a barge loaded with soldiers, and steamed away . . . . Jack's diary records: "Aug. 23rd. Heat awful. Pringle died today." He was the third soldier to succumb.

We resigned ourselves to the dreadful heat, and at the end of two more days the river had begun to narrow, and we arrived at Fort Yuma . . . . It was said to be the very hottest place that ever existed . . . . We left two companies of the regiment there. When we departed, (now aboard the paddle-wheeler Gila) I felt, somehow, as though we were saying good-bye to the world and civilization.

And now began our real journey up the Colorado River . . . with the barge full of soldiers towing on after us, starting for Fort Mohave, some two hundred miles above . . . .

One morning Jack came excitedly in and said: "Martha,

(Above) *Gold seekers often traveled to the Colorado River camps via shallow-draft steamboats that plied the river from 1852 to 1907 from Yuma Crossing to today's Bullhead City and beyond.*
ARIZONA HISTORICAL FOUNDATION
(Facing Page) *The Arizona Territorial Prison at Yuma, now preserved as a state park, confined about 3,000 outlaws from 1879 to 1909.*
PHILIP VARNEY

we are coming to Ehrenberg!" Visions of castles on the Rhine and stories of the middle ages floated through my mind in pleasurable anticipation of seeing an interesting and beautiful place. Alas! for my ignorance. I saw but a row of low thatched hovels, perched on the edge of the ragged looking river-bank; a road ran lengthwise along, and opposite the hovels I saw a store and some more mean-looking huts of adobe . . . .

At last, on the 8th of September, we arrived at Camp Mohave, on the right bank of the river . . . . On the morning of September 10th everything in the post was astir with preparations . . . . At last the command moved out . . . . The first day's march was over a dreary country; a hot wind blew, and everything was filled with dust . . . . Although our steamboat troubles were over, our land troubles had just begun.

We reached, after a few hours' travel, the desolate place where we were to camp . . . . I cannot say that life in the army, as far as I had gone, presented any very great attractions. This, our first camp, was on the river, a little above Hardyville. Good water was there, and that was all; I had not yet learned to appreciate that. There was not a tree nor a shrub to give shade. The only thing I could see, except sky and sand, was a ruined adobe enclosure, with no roof.

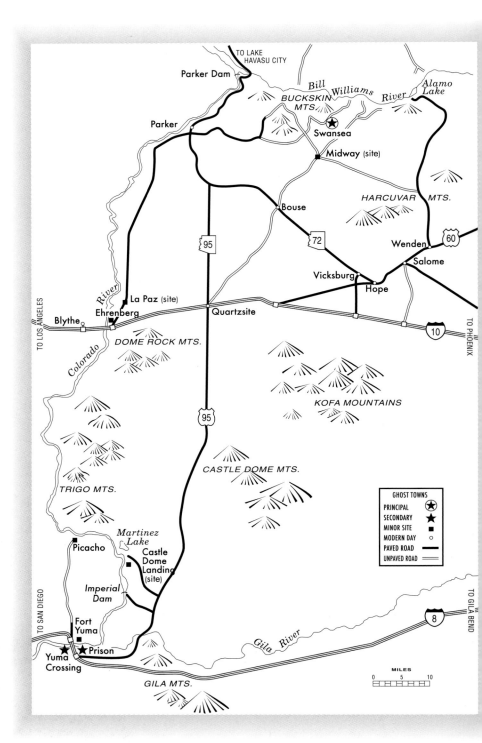

Vestiges of this era still exist along the Colorado River, from historical attractions in Yuma to upriver ghost towns. The best preserved ghost town along the river is Picacho, located in California. It is reminiscent of the many now-vanished camps and landings that dotted both sides of the Colorado before railroad bridges and dams made the water route unnavigable.

Swansea

The dusty ruin of Swansea, a premier ghost town, is situated about 4 miles south of the Bill Williams, one of west-central Arizona's largest rivers. While Swansea saw only a few good years before it was left for the desert to

(Left) *Swansea, east of Parker, is one of Arizona's premier ghost towns. The Swansea mill was the major structure in a booming town that featured theaters and restaurants, and even a car dealership in its later years.*
SHARLOT HALL MUSEUM
(Below) *The Bureau of Land Management has restored roofs to these quarters for unmarried miners at Swansea.*
PHILIP VARNEY

reclaim, its remains are eerie and intriguing. The town site is not dotted with shops, as are Jerome, Oatman, and Bisbee. Instead, Swansea is an abandoned wreck of its former self, deserted in the middle of nowhere.

Today, the site features the brick walls of a large smelter, a double row of gray-plastered, single-men's quarters, two cemeteries, the adobe walls of mining offi-cials' homes, a company store foundation, a train depot, and dump sites of the mine, mill, and smelter. Another 4 miles north on a tortuous four-wheel-drive trail brings you to the Bill Williams River and the remnants of the pumping plant that once supplied Swansea's water. All this only hints at the town's original size.

The site is managed by the federal Bureau of Land

Management, which established the Swansea Town Site Special Management Area in an attempt to stop vandalism and deterioration. In partnership with the Friends of Swansea, Inc., the BLM has carefully restored roofs to some buildings, including the single-men's quarters, and shored up others. The BLM also established an interpretive trail and installed two vault toilets for visitors.

It is difficult to imagine that this site once boasted theaters, restaurants, saloons, barbershops, and even an automobile dealership. The showplace residence was a two-story, 3,600-square-foot adobe home with a palm-tree-lined entrance.

As was often the case in early mining towns, the men who worked in the mines lived in the shadow of those civilized elements. They were primarily Mexicans and Colorado River Indians, people not welcome in the theaters and unlikely to patronize a car dealership.

The area was first prospected in 1886 by three men who were disappointed when the veins showed principally copper and only small amounts of silver. Ten years later, one of the men returned with new partners because copper was becoming more valuable. Still, little actual mining took place due to the high cost of transporting ore from such a remote place.

Then, in 1904, a rail line was proposed from Congress (see p. 31) to Parker, along the Colorado River and into California. By the time the Arizona & California Railroad was completed in 1907, claims had been consolidated in the region as the Clara Gold and Copper Company, and a mining camp began to grow.

Unfortunately for Swansea, George Mitchell, a metallurgist and the principal promoter for the mining company, was a better promoter than he was a metallurgist. He poured money into embellishments that impressed investors rather than into improvements that enhanced the mining of ore. As a result, the cost of producing copper was 3 cents per pound higher than its selling price.

As mining expert Harvey Weed wrote in his 1913 *Mines Handbook*, Mitchell's vision of Swansea was "an example of enthusiasm run wild, coupled with reckless stock selling and the foolish construction of surface works before the development of enough ore to keep them busy."

Mitchell left Swansea in 1916 to join another operation. After Mitchell's departure, or perhaps because of it, Swansea managed to make a profit for two years. Ironically, Mitchell's smelter did not process the ore — it was sent to Clarkdale, Humboldt, and Sasco (all featured in this book).

Swansea's short-lived prosperity ended after World War I when copper prices plummeted. By 1937 the town was a thoroughly scavenged ghost.

Although other mining camps have more substantial ruins and are much easier to reach, Swansea's appeal is enduring. The desert can be harsh, but it can also be stunningly beautiful and serene. While it was no doubt a difficult place to live and work, it is now a marvelous place to escape the modern world. Camping out at Swansea — with no power lines, no televisions, no air conditioners and only coyotes, hummingbirds, and other wildlife as neighbors — is a rare experience indeed. Swansea has a solitude, a serenity, that makes it one of my favorite places on the planet.

WHEN YOU GO: Swansea is 25 miles northeast of Bouse. A high-clearance vehicle is required. See p. 134 for specific directions.

(**Above**) *This vertical shaft at the Swansea mine led to a copper lode that was a rich producer until after World War I. The mine had its own smelter and supported a thriving community.*
(**Below**) *Among its amenities was a dairy, the site of which is marked by a commemorative stone.*
BOTH BY RICK ODELL

(Top) *The Clara Consolidated Gold and Copper Mining Company at Swansea was at its peak in 1910. Swansea was named after the Welsh hometown of its principal promoter, George Mitchell.*
JEREMY ROWE COLLECTION

(Above) *Wide open spaces surrounded the Swansea mine managers' billets. These ruins have deteriorated considerably since this photo was taken in 1993.*

(Left) *The crumbling walls of the Swansea train depot recall a bygone era.*
BOTH BY RICK ODELL

Yuma Crossing

Crossing the Colorado River was once a formidable task. Only at the confluence of the Colorado and Gila rivers could it be done with relative ease, making this a natural place for settlement. Although the Colorado was explored by the Spanish as early as 1540, the first Spanish settlement wasn't established until 1775, when Fr. Francisco Garces, leading missionaries and accompanying soldiers, founded a mission near the junction of the rivers. Within six years the Quechan (queet-*sahn*) Indians living along the Colorado rose up against the newcomers who had mistreated them, forced Catholicism on them, and ruined their farmlands with cattle and horse grazing. Soldiers, settlers, and Fr. Garces himself — all except women and children — were killed.

A calm settled on the area for almost 50 years. That began to change in 1829 when Kit Carson arrived at what would become known as Yuma Crossing. He collected more than 2,000 pounds of beaver pelts during this trapping expedition. Carson returned on a military expedition in 1846. That year also saw the arrival of Capt. Philip St. George Cooke and the Mormon Battalion, who were charged with establishing the first wagon road across what would become southern Arizona.

Mexican and American soldiers crossed the Colorado near the site of the old Spanish mission during the Mexican War (1846-48). Argonauts heading to the California Gold Rush used the crossing so extensively that ferry businesses began competing for trade. In 1850, a U.S. military detachment of 92 men, led by Maj. Samuel Peter Heintzelman, established Camp Calhoun on a California hill overlooking the crossing. By 1852, the installation was called Fort Yuma. That year the first steamboat-load of supplies came upriver from the Gulf of California. A community sprang up on the Arizona bank opposite the fort. The first post office, established in 1857, was named Colorado City. A year later it became Arizona City. By 1866, the post office and town were officially named Yuma.

Quartermaster Depot: More important to the history of Arizona than the mission, the fort, or even the town, was the Quartermaster Depot. It was established in 1864 on the Arizona bank of the river. One could assert that it was the single most important place that ensured the settling of the Arizona Territory. Why? Because settlers could not have withstood Indian attacks without the military protection, and the military could not have established a stronghold without sufficient supplies.

The bulk of those supplies arrived via paddle wheelers from Port Isabel, Mexico, where the river empties into the Gulf of California. The supplies were distributed from Yuma. Some were sent upstream to Fort Mohave and then inland to Fort Whipple (at the territorial capital, Prescott). The majority of the supplies, however, went overland on the Gila Trail to Fort McDowell (east of present-day Phoenix), Fort Lowell (at Tucson), and as far east as western Texas. For 13 years, until the 1877 arrival of the railroad rendered river transport obsolete, the Quartermaster Depot at Yuma Crossing ensured the U.S. military would protect settlers.

Today, visitors to Yuma Crossing State Historic Park

(**Left, Above**) *Historic Yuma Crossing on the Colorado River was used by Spanish missionaries, gold-hungry 49ers, and soldiers of the Mexican and Civil wars.*
It was bridged for the railroad in 1877.
BANCROFT LIBRARY COLLECTION
(**Left, Below**) *Yuma's Quartermaster Depot supplied the soldiers who protected early Arizona settlements.*
(**Right, Above**) *The Quartermaster Depot's commanding officers occupied this now-restored residence.*
BOTH BY PHILIP VARNEY
(**Right, Below**) *The Yuma ferry was the only wagon transport across the Colorado River in 1904.*
ARIZONA HISTORICAL SOCIETY

find it an excellent place to learn about Yuma history. The peaceful, parklike retreat consists of the former depot office, a stone reservoir, a granary and corral, and the commanding officer's quarters with its separate kitchen. The latter two buildings, connected by a roofed porch, date from 1859, before the depot's establishment. They originally served as the home of shipping magnate George Alonzo Johnson, whose five steamboats (the *Cocopah, Colorado, Mohave, Nina Tilden,* and *General Jesup*) running the Colorado generated annual revenues of about $250,000. (928) 329-0471.

Fort Yuma: By 1883, six years after the arrival of the railroad, settlers no longer needed military protection. The Quartermaster Depot was closed. A year later, Fort Yuma was transferred to the Department of the Interior and then to the Quechan Indians. The site became a Catholic boarding school until 1900. Standing today at the old fort's location on the California side of the river are the St. Thomas Mission and the Quechan Indian Museum, (760) 572-0661. If planning to visit the Quechan Indian Museum, be sure to call ahead to check on hours.

Yuma Territorial Prison: Governor Anson P.K. Safford stated in 1875 that a territorial prison was needed because county jails were generally insecure, and prisoners were in close confinement, ". . . resulting injuriously to health with

scarcely the possibility for moral improvement." Two Yuma representatives to the 8th Territorial Legislature at Tucson managed to amend a bill that would have built the new penitentiary in the more centrally located, but less politically influential, settlement of Phoenix.

In 1879 prison construction began at Yuma, much of it done by the convicts themselves. The principal work details included rock quarry, adobe yard, wood yard, prison construction, kitchen, and sewing shop.

Although movies and pulp novels portrayed the Yuma Territorial Prison as a "hell hole," it was actually more commodious than most penal institutions of the time. Corporal punishment was forbidden, and only two penalties were used: Those who attempted escape were fitted with a ball and chain. Rules violators were put in the "Dark Cell," a steel cage inside a hill with no lights, no sanitation, and bread and water just once a day.

The prison was active from 1879 to 1909, when prisoners were transferred to a new facility in Florence. Yuma High School then used the prison buildings from 1910-14, thus providing the nickname they still use: the Criminals. During the Depression the buildings sheltered homeless people, many of whom had been denied entry into California. Now an Arizona state park, the Yuma Territorial Prison offers a fascinating look into a little-recounted chapter of Arizona history; (928) 783-4771.

The museum has extensive displays of photographs, artifacts, and journals of life at the prison. Rather than dry facts, they are testaments to the drama of prison life. Consider these entries:

Pathos — J.A. Cleveland, just 14 years old, served five years for robbery.

Courage — Prison inmate Barney Riggs was pardoned from a life sentence after saving prison Superintendent Thomas Gates' life during an escape attempt. He wrenched a revolver from one of the participants and killed a prisoner who was stabbing Gates.

(Left, Above) *The Yuma Territorial Prison, perched above the Colorado River at Yuma, is shown shortly before it was abandoned in 1909 for a new facility in Florence. It is now a popular tourist attraction, drawing some 140,000 visitors each year.* ARIZONA HIGHWAYS COLLECTION
(Left) *Visitors to the Yuma Territorial Prison, now a state park, peer into the dark cells and wonder what life must have been like.* JAMES TALLON
(Right, Above) *Pearl Hart, a stagecoach robber, was the most celebrated female inmate at the prison.* ARIZONA HISTORICAL SOCIETY
(Right) *While buildings at Picacho, on the California side of the Colorado River, are now crumbling, the town boasted 2,500 citizens at the turn of the century.* JAMES TALLON

Humor — Although serving a 15-month sentence for forgery, one-time Phoenix Public Schools Superintendent R.L. McDonald was put in charge of the prisoners' accounts. When he was released, McDonald left with $130 of their money.

Tragedy — Single mother Isabella Washington, one of 29 women to serve time at Yuma prison, was sent here for throwing her newborn baby into an irrigation canal near Tempe.

Lesson for Holding One's Tongue — Edward Lopez was serving five years for grand larceny when he bragged of killing 19 people in Mexico. He was extradited to that country in the company of six Mexican officers who, once they crossed the border, shot Lopez to death, expending exactly 19 bullets.

Sign of the Times — Feliciano Gomez, serving 10 years for assault to commit murder, spent four separate sentences in the dreaded Dark Cell for gambling in prison and was once penalized further for refusing to give up his dice. Nowadays he would be an honored guest in Laughlin or Las Vegas.

WHEN YOU GO: The Yuma Crossing Quartermaster Depot is north of the intersection of First Street and Second Avenue in north-central Yuma. The Territorial Prison is east of Interstate 8 off the Giss Parkway Exit.

Picacho and the Vanished River Ghosts

Picacho, located just across the Colorado River in California, is a unique site. It is the lone survivor of the damming of the river that eliminated virtually everything but the memory of several once-important communities along the Colorado's banks. Picacho Peak (which translates from Spanish to an English redundancy, "Peak Peak") rises more than 1,300 feet above the surrounding desert. Beneath it is the Picacho Mine, worked intermittently since placer deposits were discovered in 1862.

Beginning in 1878, several entrepreneurs tried to organize the Picacho claims to build a paying operation. By 1902, the site was an "oasis of bustle," according to the *Los Angeles Times*. The mine freighted gold ore some 5 miles north to a riverside mill and townsite originally known as El Rio and, later, as Picacho.

Eventually Picacho had a population estimated at 2,500, but its peak years were few. In 1904 a belt broke at the mill, causing a 21-ton flywheel to break loose and catapult through the roof. While the building sustained severe structural damage, there were, remarkably, no deaths. Only two weeks later, a rainstorm washed out the

narrow-gauge railroad that took ore from the mine. Then gold prices declined. Finally, the completion of Laguna Dam in 1909 ended river navigation and the cheap transportation of ore. As a parting insult, water behind the dam submerged much of Picacho. Despite attempts to reopen the mines in the 1930s, the town was dead.

The majority of visitors to Picacho come to camp, picnic, or fish at Picacho State Recreation Area. For the ghost town hunter, there are three reasons to take the hour's drive from Yuma to Picacho: the cemetery, the historical tour, and the extraordinary scenery.

Located southwest of the ranger station, the cemetery was moved from its original spot, which is now submerged by the waters of the Colorado. Neat rows of graves are surrounded by a white picket fence that looks better suited to the Vermont countryside.

The Picacho Mills Historic Tour, a 2-mile round-trip hike that takes about 90 minutes, combines both history and scenery. To reach the trailhead, take the right turn after the park entrance and continue toward the ranger residences. Stop at the turnout for a brochure. The hike features the Picacho cave jail, remnants of two mills, wonderful views of the Colorado River, and a geologist's dream of natural colors and formations. Interestingly, while Picacho is in California, the river bends so that Arizona surrounds it to the north, east, and south.

WHEN YOU GO: From Yuma, cross into California on Interstate 8 and take the Winterhaven exit. Before reaching Winterhaven, turn right onto Picacho Road and follow signs directing you to the Picacho State Recreation Area 23 miles away. The last 13 miles to the mine are unpaved, as are the 4 miles beyond the mine to the townsite. The trip requires a high-clearance vehicle. This is a fair-weather trip only, as the last 3 miles are within a normally dry wash. (760) 996-2963.

Castle Dome Landing began in 1864 after prospectors in the Castle Dome Mountains found evidence of earlier mines, which they thought to be Spanish. Once a community of about 50 people downriver from Picacho, the site is now beneath the water behind Imperial Dam.

Ehrenberg is the Arizona neighbor to Blythe, California. It was settled in 1867 and named for surveyor Herman Ehrenberg. By the mid-1870s the town had a population of about 500 and featured a hotel, a bakery, and a stage station. It was doomed, as were many upriver towns, by the arrival in 1877 of the railroad in Yuma and the 1909 construction of Laguna Dam, which blocked river ports north of the dam from Yuma and the sea.

The only historic spot to visit in present-day Ehrenberg is the old cemetery, located .3 of a mile west of the I-10 exit into town. In 1935, the Arizona State Highway Department erected a marker honoring pioneers to the territory. More than 100 graves remain, including that of Filipe Gonzales. Next to it lies the broken frame of the wagon he brought to Ehrenberg from Fort Yuma in 1892.

La Paz, once about 7 miles north of Ehrenberg, today shows nothing of antiquity. Founded in 1862, this river port and mining center held the Yuma County seat until 1871. But its placer gold gave out and the river changed course, removing the port's only reasons for existence. About 1910, the river jumped its banks and destroyed the adobe remains of what had already become a ghostly town.

Quartzsite, located 18 miles east of Ehrenberg on I-10, has a cemetery that contains numerous pioneer graves. Among them is the monument for Hadji Ali (1829-1902), the Syrian-born camel driver, packer, and scout who came to the U.S. in 1856 as chief camel driver for trailblazer Lt. Edward Beale (see p. 36). The soldiers simplified Hadji Ali to "Hi Jolly," but to his Quartzsite neighbors he was known as Philip Tedro. After the Beale expedition, Ali kept several of the camels, eventually releasing them in 1868. For years startled Arizonans reported sighting camels in the desert.

Other once-prominent Colorado River ports north of Ehrenberg and La Paz that have disappeared include Aubrey Landing, located at the confluence of the Bill Williams and Colorado rivers and now submerged under Lake Havasu; Hardyville, absorbed and overrun by Bullhead City; and Polhamus Landing, near the present site of Davis Dam, north of Bullhead City.

(Above) *The elements have severely eroded the wagon that Filipe Gonzales drove northward from Fort Yuma in 1892. It rests today at the Ehrenberg cemetery.*
PHILIP VARNEY
(Right) *This nugget of gold on quartz, mined in Pima County is on display at the Arizona Mining and Mineral Museum.*
JOHN DREW

Arizona Ghost Towns

COLOR PORTFOLIO

& Mining Camps

58

(Left) *Once hailed as "the billion-dollar copper camp," Jerome still perches precariously on Cleopatra Hill. Many who were residents during Jerome's boisterous heydays rest in the old cemetery.*

(Top) *The panorama of the Verde Valley is spectacular from Jerome's James S. Douglas Mansion, lower right in the photo. The shell of the Little Daisy Hotel, now partially restored as a residence, is visible to the left of the mansion.*

(Above) *Mine vehicles and other equipment that forged Jerome's place in mining history are on display at the Mine Museum and Douglas mansion.*
ALL BY JOHN DREW

(Right) *An outstanding example of malachite, a copper ore.*
JERRY JACKA

(Right, Top) *Cleator began its slow decline when the mines closed in the 1920s. Town owner and namesake Jimmy Cleator put his once-vibrant ranching and mining town up for sale in 1949 but had no takers.*
(Right, Below) *In addition to its intriguing gravesites, the Crown King cemetery is noted for its mountain solitude.*
BOTH BY PHILIP VARNEY
(Far Right, Below) *The Senator Mine, south of Prescott, started producing gold in 1864 and later had some production of silver and copper. The road past it is known as the Senator Highway, but it's really too primitive to rate that name.*
ROBERT J. FARRELL
(Following Panel, Pages 62-63) *Vulture Mine, one of the richest gold caches in the state's history, supplied bullion to the Union army during the Civil War.*
JEFF KIDA

(Above) *When the mines closed, Jerome's population of 15,000 dwindled to just a few hardy souls. The town has since been reborn as a thriving mecca for artists, retirees, and tourists.*
(Right) *The promise of filling pans with gold drew hordes of prospectors to Yavapai County streams.*
BOTH BY JOHN DREW

(**Facing Page**) *Yesteryear is preserved for today's visitors at the Vulture Mine. This is the well-equipped assay office where ore from one of Arizona's richest gold mines was tested.*
JOHN DREW

(**Left**) *The gold strike at Rich Hill (seen in the background) lured thousands of prospectors to the area in the 1860s. These remains of a stone dwelling are near the abandoned town of Octave.*
JERRY JACKA

(**Below**) *Crucibles such as these were used to assay ore.*
JOHN DREW

(**Bottom**) *These scattered structures are all that is left of the mining community of Humbug, named for a promising creek that proved to harbor little gold.*
PHILIP VARNEY

Some lucky placer miner found this gold, now on display at the Arizona Mining and Mineral Museum in Phoenix.
JOHN DREW

(Above) *A strategically painted crosswalk leads patrons between two bars in historic Chloride.*
JOHN DREW
(Above, Left) *The town of Oatman, along historic U.S. Route 66, has survived mine closings and is a favorite stop for seekers of Old West flavor.*
JERRY JACKA
(Left) *Little is left of Goldroad, whose mines produced $17 million worth of gold between 1899 and 1907. The site was razed in 1949 to reduce taxes.*
JOHN DREW

The setting sun provides a glorious backdrop for the headframe of the Golden Gem Mine at Cerbat. Headframes anchored the cables that lowered workers in cages into the vertical shafts and raised ore in buckets. Cerbat was the seat of Mohave County from 1871 to 1873.
JOHN DREW

(**Above**) *Remnants of numerous tiny mining camps are strewn along the Colorado River, where several gold strikes created brief booms in the 1860s. Today most are accessible only by boat. These stone walls once enclosed the mill at Picacho.*
JAMES TALLON

(**Right**) *Theaters, restaurants, shops, and even an automobile dealership once thrived near the now-crumbling Swansea railroad depot.*
RICK ODELL

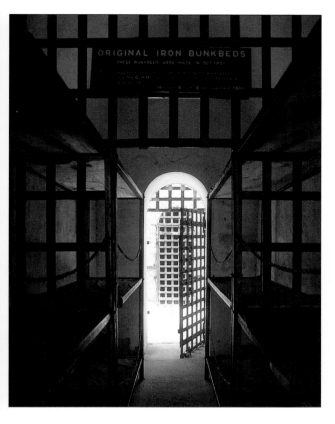

(**Left**) *Although considered modern at the time, the Arizona Territorial Prison at Yuma, now preserved as a state park, could never have been mistaken for a country club.*
JAMES TALLON
(**Below**) *Little was missed from the guard tower, which overlooks the prison walls on one side and the Colorado River on another.*
JOHN DREW

(Left) *Clifton, the only surviving territorial town along Chase Creek, boasts some of the best-preserved Victorian structures in the state.*
JOHN DREW

(Below) *The arrival in 1884 of the narrow-gauge Arizona and New Mexico Railroad enhanced Clifton's mining stature. The restored 1913 train depot is a vivid reminder of the town's glory days.*
PHILIP VARNEY

(Above) *With its tracks just 20 inches apart, the Coronado Railroad was a "baby gauge" line whose first cars were pulled up by mule and returned by gravity. Its subsequent engine, the "Copper Head," is on display in Clifton.*

(Right) *Azurite is common in Arizona copper mines. This specimen is among the many interesting exhibits at the Arizona Mining and Mineral Museum in Phoenix.*
BOTH BY JOHN DREW

*The 20-room Sibley Mansion at Copper
Creek was built in 1908, and was
considered one of the Territory's finest
showplaces. The Copper Creek mines closed
in 1917, reopened in 1933, then closed
for good in 1942.*
PHILIP VARNEY

(Top) *For decades the privately owned Santa Cruz County town of Ruby was posted with "no trespassing" signs. Now guided tours take ghost town enthusiasts through the many standing structures of the century-old settlement.* JOHN DREW

(Above) *Gold! This pouchful was enough to grubstake a prospector to months of arduous searching in unfriendly terrain.* JERRY JACKA

(Left) *Montana Peak dominates the landscape around the remains of once-turbulent Ruby.*

(Following Panel, Pages 74-75) *Though its tumultuous history includes several raids by bandits, Ruby is restful and quiet today. Perhaps as a result of being closed to the public for decades, several buildings survive, including the mill foundations, the assay office, and the warehouse, left to right in the sunshine in this panorama.* BOTH BY JOHN DREW

(Facing Page) *Miners' quarters in Pearce were never much to look at. Nor were they intended to endure. Because its roof survived to protect it, this one has outlasted its neighbors built of adobe.*
(Left) *The Courtland jail is the only roofed structure left from the days when Courtland had such highfalutin' amenities as a movie theater, an ice cream parlor, its own newspaper, and an automobile dealership.*
BOTH BY JERRY JACKA
(Below) *This silver ore was extracted from the Sierrita Mountains of Pima County.*
JOHN DREW
(Bottom) *The image of the arched entrance to the Gleeson schoolhouse is preserved in this photograph. The arch has since fallen.*
JERRY JACKA

77

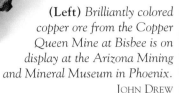

(Left) *Brilliantly colored copper ore from the Copper Queen Mine at Bisbee is on display at the Arizona Mining and Mineral Museum in Phoenix.* JOHN DREW
(Below) *Tombstone regularly reenacts its Old West history with staged gunfights on historic Allen Street.* INGE MARTIN

(Top) *Legendary Tombstone has preserved its past with meticulous care. The Territorial courthouse, a special jewel, was built during the turbulent 1880s. Still, some disputes likely were settled in the town's rough-and-tumble streets in favor of the man with the fastest draw.* JERRY JACKA
(Above) *Visitors from around the world flock to Tombstone to see the OK Corral, site of the 1881 Earp-Clanton shootout.*
(Right) *Bisbee takes great pride in its lovingly restored historic buildings, some of which give it the air of turn-of-the-century San Francisco. This house is at the foot of Castle Rock.* BOTH BY JOHN DREW

The restored Copper Queen Hotel, Bisbee's most celebrated hostelry, still welcomes guests. The start of the Queen Mine Tour and the Mining Museum are nearby.
JERRY JACKA

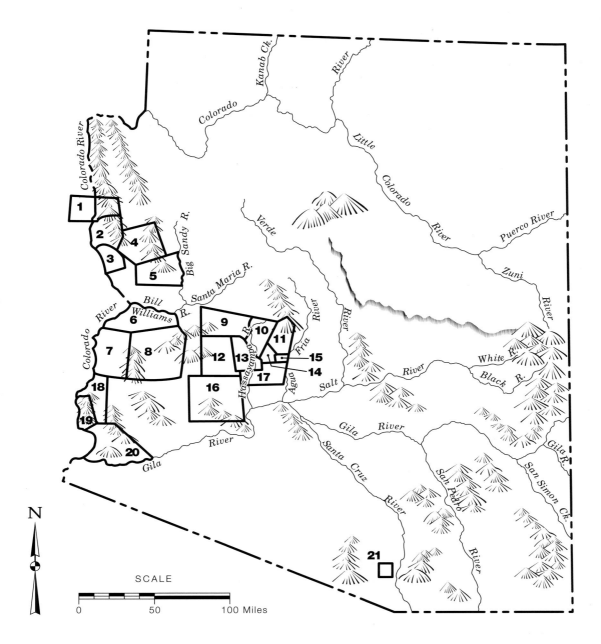

MINING DISTRICTS

Mining Districts were self-governing units of miners that predated the territorial government.
Boundaries of the organized districts are shown as they existed in 1866.

1. **El Dorado Cañon**
2. **Pyramid**
3. **San Francisco**
4. **Sacramento**
5. **Waubau Yuma**
6. **Williams Fork**
7. **La Paz**

8. **Harcuvar**
9. **Yavapai**
10. **Hassayampa**
11. **Big Bug**
12. **Weaver**
13. **Walnut Grove**
14. **Turkey Creek**

15. **Bradshaw**
16. **Wickenburg**
17. **Agua Fria**
18. **Weaver**
19. **Eureka**
20. **Castle Dome**
21. **Cerro Colorado**

(Facing Page) *Bisbee's unique Victorian architecture,*
moderate mile-high climate, and rich history lure an
increasing number of visitors each year.
JOHN DREW

CHAPTER 5

Ghosts of Copper Country

In the area bounded by Superior on the west and the New Mexico border on the east, copper has been paying off for well over a century. While giant operations still flourish at Oak Flat, Kearny, Globe-Miami, and Morenci, dozens of waste dumps, test holes, abandoned mining camps, and ghost towns also dot these areas — reminders of mining's fickle nature. Unfortunately, many of these ghost towns stood in the way of larger operations. The towns of Sonora, Ray, Metcalf, Old Morenci, and Christmas were among those swallowed by ever-widening open pits or covered by waste dumps.

But there is still much to see. The four sites featured here offer considerable variety: Clifton, with dozens of decaying buildings that delight photographers, is one of the most complete mining towns profiled in this book; Klondyke and Cochran, while offering fewer buildings, are located in beautiful settings; and Copper Hill is a prime example of what remains when a mining operation shuts down, salvages everything of value, and moves on.

Clifton, Old Morenci, and Metcalf

The story of three Greenlee County mining camps begins with an exciting mineral discovery, continues with the establishment of two major copper companies, and ends with an even larger company — Phelps Dodge — engulfing the other two. In the tale's postscript, two of the three mining camps disappear into a vast open pit, leaving only historic Clifton.

First came a soldier's chance discovery. It was a promising find, and Bob Metcalf vowed he'd return to take a closer look. It was about 1866, and Metcalf was on a mission with other Union soldiers to recover cavalry horses stolen by Apache warriors. They followed the horses' trail from the Gila River up along the San Francisco River and into a steep, narrow canyon. That's when Metcalf saw the copper.

Bob and his brother Jim came back to the canyon years later, named the stream "Chase Creek" in honor of the captain who led them on that fortuitous mission, and filed the Metcalf claims. They called their first mine the

(**Above**) *Flooding of the San Francisco River, like this occurrence in 1884, has brought devastation to Clifton on several occasions.*
ARIZONA STATE LIBRARY, ARCHIVES AND PUBLIC RECORDS
(**Facing Page**) *Clifton and the Chase Creek Historic District provide a cornucopia of architectural delights for the ghost town buff.*
JOHN DREW

Longfellow, reportedly because they discovered the ore on the poet's birthday. It turned out to be the first mine to tap into one of the richest, longest-lasting copper deposits in the United States. Nevertheless, the Metcalf claims were sold to the Leszinsky brothers in 1872.

As mining activity in the area increased, two communities formed along Chase Creek — Clifton and Morenci, later to be joined by the town of Metcalf.

The first camp grew up around the site of the Leszinsky brothers' adobe smelter. Located at the confluence of Chase Creek and the San Francisco River, it became known as Clifton. This was either a shortening of "Cliff Town," referring to the surrounding cliffs, or a nod to Henry Clifton, Yavapai County recorder who had prospected the area as early as 1864.

The second community was Joy's Camp, named for miner William Joy, who also had phenomenal claims in the area. However, three problems caused Joy to eventually discontinue work: no reliable smelter, the prohibitive price of ore transportation, and the constant threat of Indian attack. William Church came to the area in 1875 and organized the Detroit Copper Company to take over the Joy claims. To consolidate operations, Church moved the town 7 miles to the mine site and changed the name from Joy's Camp to Morenci, after a town in his native Michigan. Legend says Morenci was situated on hillsides so steep that mothers kept their children on tethers to prevent them from falling out of their yards.

The Leszinsky brothers, meanwhile, in order to get ore from their mine to the smelting site in Clifton 4 miles away, constructed one of Arizona's most intriguing railroads, the Coronado. It was a "baby gauge" line, with tracks only 20 inches apart.

Originally the line had no locomotives. Mules hauled empty cars up to the mine site. When the cars were filled with ore, the mules were returned via special platforms built on the cars. Gravity provided locomotion from mine to smelter. Derailments were of little concern because the cars were so small they could be righted and placed back on the tracks by hand. The first locomotive for the Coronado line was built in Baltimore, shipped by rail to Colorado, and brought by wagon to Clifton in 1879. Another was shipped around the Horn to San Francisco. From there a second ship took it to Port Isabel, Mexico, where it was put on a paddle wheeler to travel

up the Colorado River to Yuma and overland to Clifton.

Back in Morenci, the Detroit Copper Company needed money for a smelter. Church, in 1881, arranged to borrow $50,000 — big money in those days — from a

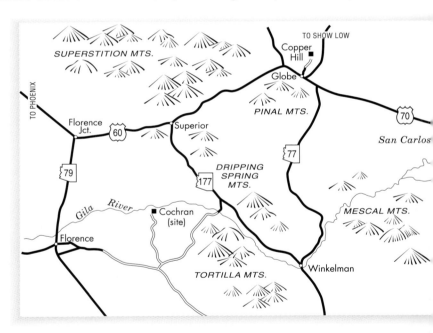

New York city mercantile and trading company. Thus Phelps Dodge entered into mining, a field in which it would become world-renowned.

In 1882 the Scottish-owned Arizona Copper Company bought out the Leszinsky brothers and extended the Coronado Railroad 3 more miles from Clifton to the community of Metcalf (which eventually had a population of about 5,000). Clifton became even more significant to the mining district in 1884 with the arrival of the narrow-gauge Arizona and New Mexico Railroad, an

(Far Left) *Chase Street in Clifton was a busy shopping thoroughfare in 1910, offering a greater selection of goods and services than most Arizona towns.*
JEREMY ROWE COLLECTION
(Left) *The only survivor of the three Chase Creek camps, Clifton still has a solidity and permanence that is rare in most century-old mining communities.*
PHILIP VARNEY

extension from Lordsburg on the Southern Pacific Railroad. As both a smelting site and a direct rail link for the Arizona Copper Company, Clifton developed a look of permanence, with buildings filling the canyon along Chase Creek.

Phelps Dodge, in 1897, took over the remainder of Detroit Mining Company stock from William Church for $1.6 million. Another major power shift occurred in 1921 when Phelps Dodge bought out the Arizona Copper Company, leaving the Clifton-Morenci-Metcalf miners with a single employer.

Operations prospered until 1932, when the Depression caused the mines to shut down. Five years later, a new era of mining began along Chase Creek. New technology marked the end of underground mining and the beginning of the open pit, which continues to this day.

For ghost town enthusiasts, open-pit mining was the beginning of the end. The town of Metcalf disappeared as

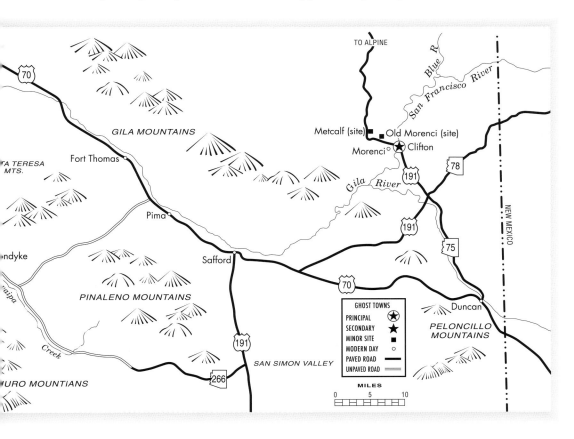

the pit expanded; even the cemetery was moved. Old Morenci, which once featured some of the finest buildings in the state, was spared until the early 1970s. As a new Morenci was built three miles closer to Clifton, Old Morenci vanished into the pit.

While Clifton is the only surviving town of the original three mining camps along Chase Creek, survival hasn't been easy. The county seat since the establishment of Greenlee County in 1909, Clifton endured disastrous floods in 1906 and 1983, a fire that destroyed much of the business district in 1913, and at least two bitter labor disputes.

The first labor strike occurred in 1903 when the territory's entire deployment of Arizona Rangers and National Guard, augmented by more than 800 Army regulars, curtailed the activities of striking miners. The workers eventually agreed to the company's terms. Strike leader William "Three Finger Jack" Loustauneau was fined $2,000 and sentenced to two years at the Yuma

(Above) *The Cliff Jail in Clifton was hewn out of solid rock. The miner who fashioned it was its first inmate.*
JOHN DREW
(Facing Page, Above) *The Morenci Hotel, in the town of the same name, was one of the Arizona Territory's most luxurious hostelries in 1905.*
ARIZONA STATE LIBRARY, ARCHIVES AND PUBLIC RECORDS
(Facing Page, Below) *Metcalf, now swallowed along with Old Morenci by an open-pit mine, once was a thriving town. The large building seen at the left was the Arizona Copper Company store.*
ARIZONA HIGHWAYS COLLECTION

Territorial Prison for illegal activities. He never made it out alive. Because of his belligerence, Loustauneau was moved to the "incorrigible ward." He attempted escape and assaulted both the penitentiary superintendent and the superintendent's assistant. "Three Finger Jack" later died of heat prostration in 1906.

A second strike, in 1983, was marked by statewide headlines, gunshots, the presence of the National Guard, and the decertification of the unions. Anger still festers in many Clifton homes.

Today Clifton has only two Arizona rivals for significant historic buildings and other ghost town attractions: Jerome and Bisbee. But those towns strut their stuff. Clifton is different. You have to get off the highway and explore the town to see its treasures. In Clifton, the past hides in the present.

In a 1992 edition of *The Journal of Arizona History*, architect Mark Vinson, a native of the area, described the four dozen structures of Clifton's Chase Creek business district: "Arches, balconies, and Victorian and Neoclassical detailing, combined with the narrow street, dense one- and two-story facades, and the natural setting, give Chase Creek an ambiance unequaled anywhere in the state."

The best field guide to Chase Creek is a walking tour brochure written by Clifton native Charles O. Spezia. Request a copy at the Greenlee County Historical Society, located in the 1913 Eagle Hall. Many of the buildings along Chase Creek, including Eagle Hall, were built by Antonio and Ambrose Spezia, entrepreneurs who constructed not just places of business, but edifices with beauty and character. Their vision made an indelible contribution to Clifton's atmosphere.

The historical society has created several informative displays of Clifton-Morenci-Metcalf memorabilia. One is a 1915 model of the area that shows mines, smelters, railroads, and the locations of now-vanished places like Old Morenci and Metcalf.

In addition to Eagle Hall, other buildings worth examining along Chase Creek include the Sacred Heart Catholic Church, the Palicio House, and the Cascarelli Building, with the shell of the Alhambra Theater next door.

The parking area for Chase Creek is across the street from a convenience market that stands where the Coronado Railroad terminus met the Leszinskys' smelter. The steep walls of the canyon above the market still show the railroad bed that was carved out of the rock.

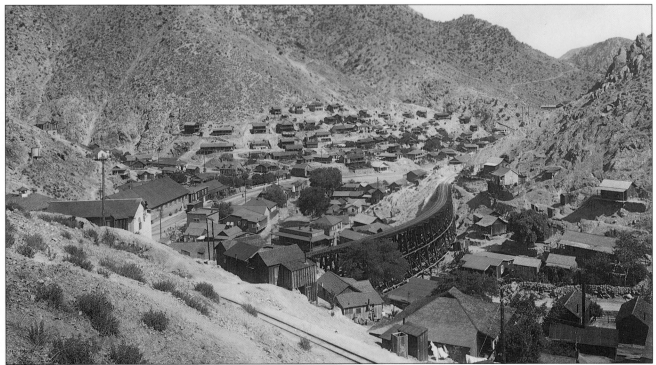

South of Chase Creek, along the highway, is the exquisitely restored 1913 train depot. This brick structure, with its red tile roof, has wide overhanging eaves — so wide, in fact, that when the adjacent highway was widened, a corner of the roof had to be lopped off.

Across the street from the depot is a baby gauge locomotive from the old Coronado line (a second stands at the shopping plaza in new Morenci). Next to the engine is the old Cliff Jail, a two-cell bastille carved out of solid rock that makes the Yuma Territorial Prison look like a Hilton.

The Greenlee County Courthouse, built in 1911, stands in South Clifton, which was originally known as Hill's Addition — Clifton's first subdivision. The once-stately edifice has lost most of its spacious lawn and sloping steps, so it now appears to have been stuffed into far too small a place. Also in South Clifton is the 1928 bath house, which sits across the San Francisco River from the train depot. Built in the Spanish Colonial Revival style, the bathhouse looks as if it could have been lifted bodily from Balboa Park in San Diego. Down the street is the

deteriorating Central Hotel, constructed of blocks made from poured smelter slag.

One of Arizona's loveliest early residences, now a bed and breakfast, is hidden away 2.5 miles north of Clifton. Take Frisco Road, which crosses the San Francisco River on the Polly Rosenbaum Bridge, north out of town. Delbert Maxwell Potter was a self-taught lawyer and gold-mine owner. In 1901 he commissioned the building of a showplace residence. Situated on 60 acres that once featured well-kept gardens and 1,800 fruit and ornamental trees, the house has 18-inch-thick adobe walls and 10-foot-high ceilings. The three-bedroom home, which was

damaged in the 1983 flood and devastated by subsequent vandalism, has been carefully restored by Potter's granddaughter, June Palmer, who was born in the house in a bed her mother still owns. The extraordinary Potter Ranch home was registered as a National Historic Landmark in 1978.

Four cemeteries serve as reminders of Clifton, Old Morenci, and Metcalf, but visitors have to search to find them. Once more, the past hides in the present.

The graves of the old Metcalf Cemetery were moved to a site above Clifton near a current Catholic cemetery and an unused ball field. Another cemetery is near the highway heading north from town. Just past a haul-road stoplight, more than 100 untended graves extend up a hillside. The Clifton Cemetery is just shy of 3 miles southeast of town on Ward Canyon Road. One of the largest stones marks the Potter family plot, but only one grave is there — that of Lizzie Potter (1860-1917). It reads, "Always loving, faithful and true — sweetheart, wife, and mother." The stone was placed by "Dell" Potter, owner of Potter Ranch.

The best-preserved cemetery in the Clifton-Morenci area is hidden in the present, indeed. Although inside the current Phelps Dodge operation, it is open to the public. Drive through Morenci to the Phelps Dodge gate and ask to visit the Bunker Cemetery. Its Italian cypress trees and other foliage are visible from the guard station.

Bunker Cemetery is an anomaly, a serene and holy piece of Old Clifton and Morenci completely dwarfed by waste dumps, machinery, and two huge smokestacks. Despite modern surroundings, it provides a picture window to view the past. Several graves are in marked-off sections, such as those of fraternal organizations. Other areas seem to be ethnically grouped. One large section of at least 150 graves was undoubtedly a potter's field, as almost all graves are unmarked and untended. The most interesting tombstones are the graves of Italians in the northwest section. Elaborate wrought-iron fences mark off family or individual plots; many stones are beautifully carved. Here lie many members of the pioneer Spezia family, including Antonio (1865-1940) and Ambrose (1866-1946), the brothers who left us the architectural legacy of historic Chase Creek.

WHEN YOU GO: Clifton is 207 miles southeast of Phoenix or 159 miles northeast of Tucson.

Additional Sites

Klondyke was founded near the turn of the century by prospectors who had returned from Klondike and the Yukon Territory gold rush. They apparently hoped that naming their new home after a bonanza might bring them luck. Perhaps to give the place a little individuality, or perhaps because they couldn't spell, the town — along with the neighboring butte, mountain, and wash — was called Klondyke and spelled with a "y."

Although gold was what the prospectors sought, silver and lead were what they found. The principal mines in the vicinity were the Grand Reef and the Aravaipa, although my favorite mine name is the Dog Water. You can almost hear someone ask, "Your ore showin' any color?" And the reply, "It ain't showin' dog water."

In addition to mining, the Klondyke region attracted ranchers. Its population peaked at about 500. The first commercial enterprises were owned by a Mr. Bedoya, who started a mercantile out of a tent. He then built a store and a saloon out of lumber. John F. Greenwood bought the store in about 1904 and opened a post office within his business, serving as the town's first postmaster from 1907-1917. When the store burned down, Greenwood built another out of adobe to replace it. In addition to businesses, the town had a school and a community church.

The Depression cut the town's population by half. The post office closed in 1955. By the mid-1980s only two dozen or so people lived in Klondyke. But what a place to live! Like some other ghost towns featured in this book, there isn't much left to see, yet the remains stand in absolutely glorious surroundings. Set in the lovely Aravaipa Valley with a creek of the same name running through it, Klondyke is surrounded by the rugged Galiuro Mountains to the southwest and the Santa Teresa Mountains to the north. Because Klondyke's next door neighbor is the Aravaipa Wilderness Area, the town is extremely peaceful. People don't go through Klondyke to get somewhere else (unless they're going hiking or bird-watching). Those who visit Klondyke, and certainly those who live here, are predisposed to love it.

For the ghost town buff, Klondyke still yields rewards. The adobe general store, which has gone through several owners, remains open daily between 10 A.M. and 6 P.M. for business and conversation. In addition to basic foodstuffs, the store features the original post office boxes. A nondescript building down the street formerly was the school. Farther north up the road about 1.5 miles, on fenced-off private property, are the community church and considerable remnants of the mill that once processed ore for mines in the area.

Southeast of town is the Klondyke

(**Above**) *Klondyke's general store and post office, pictured in 1910, served both miners and ranchers.*
ARIZONA HISTORICAL SOCIETY
(**Right**) *This building at the Klondyke Mine mill most likely served as the dining hall.*
(**Facing Page**) *The Potter Ranch residence north of Clifton, built in 1901, has been restored and is now a bed-and-breakfast establishment.*
BOTH BY PHILIP VARNEY

Cemetery, the resting place of Thomas Jefferson "Jeff" Power, his wife, daughter, and two of his three sons. This is one of southeastern Arizona's most notorious stories, carrying with it elements of Old West tragedy. Jeff Power brought his family from Texas to Arizona in 1909 to found a cattle ranch. In 1915, Power's wife Martha Jane was killed in a runaway horse-and-buggy accident. A year later, Power took his children into the hills to mine a claim in the Galiuro Mountains. There they constructed a cabin in Rattlesnake Canyon. In 1917 daughter Ola May died of poisoning. Charley, Power's eldest son, was turned down when he attempted to enlist during World War I. The old man determined his other sons, John and Tom Jr., were not to become cannon fodder either and forbade them to register for the draft. They were declared evaders, and on February 10, 1918, four Graham County lawmen were sent to arrest the brothers. By the time the shooting stopped, three of the four lawmen and the senior Power were dead. Brothers Tom and John, despite being wounded, made it to Mexico but were captured, extradited, tried, and convicted of murder. Then 28 and 26, respectively, they were sent to the state prison in Florence. Their brother Charley left the country.

The Power brothers were released from prison in 1960, after serving 42 years. John returned to the Klondyke area. According to John, Tom was poisoned in Los Angeles and died in 1970 in Sunset, Arizona, (about 47 road miles south of Klondyke). John retrieved the remains of his father from the site of his death at the

cabin and moved them to the Klondyke Cemetery. He put the following on the marker: "T.J. Power Sr. 1918 — Age 54. Shot down with his hands up in his own door." He placed the graves of his father and brother next to his mother and sister. Now John has joined them in the Klondyke Cemetery.

In some quarters of Aravaipa Valley a strong sentiment remains that the whole Power tragedy had little to do with draft evasion and a lot to do with the authorities' general antipathy toward the Power family and even, perhaps, a desire to take over their mining claims.

WHEN YOU GO: Klondyke is 42 miles west of Safford. Under normal conditions, the roads are suitable for passenger cars.

Copper Hill, north of Globe, once was surrounded by mines. It all began during that area's boom about 1873, which caused hopeful prospectors to spread out in all directions. A nearby canyon showed only marginal promise and was overlooked for many years. But not long after the turn of the century, four mines there began producing paying ore: the Boston, Iron Cap, Superior, and Arizona Commercial. They were situated around Copper Hill, and the community that grew near the workings took the same name. A post office was established in 1908. By 1925, the town had a population of about 500 and featured a school and a hospital, along with the usual businesses, saloons, and homes.

But the ore bodies didn't last. By 1930 the population had dwindled to 40. The post office shut its doors in 1933, effectively closing the book on Copper Hill.

Except for some modern homes that have made Copper Hill a kind of northern suburb of Globe, only company-built ruins stand at the townsite. Buildings like miners' homes and businesses have long since been scavenged or destroyed. Heavy-duty concrete mill ruins along one hillside show evidence that everything of value has been removed, probably for scrap during World War II. Tailings dumps, foundations, and isolated walls are scattered throughout the canyon. The best ruin at Copper Hill has a sturdy vault, indicating it was probably the company office or a bank. The ruin is roofless, typical of structures that were razed to save money on taxes.

Not much of the mining company complex at Copper Hill survives today. But this concrete structure has defied the ravages of time.
PHILIP VARNEY

WHEN YOU GO: Copper Hill is north of Globe. Take Broad Street to Yuma and turn north to High Street. Take High Street west for a matter of feet to Copperhill Road. Copper Hill is 2.0 miles north of that intersection on a road suitable for cars.

Cochran was a mining and railroad town along the Phoenix and Eastern Railroad. The Silver Bell and Copper Butte mines, combined with the rail-stop trade from neighboring ranches, created a community that probably never surpassed 100 people. A post office was established in 1904 with Julian H. Henness as postmaster. The second postmaster was John S. Cochran, for whom the place was named. The town, which once had a rooming house, a mercantile, and other businesses, lost its post office in 1915. The community has virtually vanished, with only a few faint foundations visible among the trees by the railroad tracks.

What makes Cochran worth seeing, besides the desert scenery, is a spectacular bank of five charcoal "beehive" kilns standing like ancient temples on the north side of the Gila River about a half mile west of the Cochran site. The kilns are just over 30 feet high and 72 feet in circumference. They are made from native stone cut into blocks held together by decomposed granite rather than mortar. Placed on the National Registry of Historic Places in 1971, the ovens were probably constructed in 1882. An article from October of that year in the Florence *Arizona Weekly Enterprise* mentions that the Pinal Consolidated Mining Company had built large kilns in the area to turn mesquite into charcoal, which was used to smelt ore from nearby silver mines. Charcoal, which burns hotter and longer than the wood from which it is derived, was often used in the smelting process, although coke (from coal) was preferred when available. (For more on the process, consult the Walker entry, p. 23.)

William Fred Jenkins, who homesteaded on the banks of the Gila and actually lived in one of the kilns, gave a different version of their purpose. In 1938 Jenkins told Wesley B. Farley, who worked on a U.S. Land Office crew surveying the area, that the structures were not kilns at all, but rather smelters, and that they were built by Scottish miners in the 1850s. He stated that mesquite charcoal was lit on the floor and that ore buckets were hung from hooks inside for the smelting process.

Perhaps they were used for smelting at one time, but I believe they were built as kilns, not smelters. I have seen more than 40 such structures in New Mexico, California, and Idaho. All of them, like the ones at Cochran, had a low entrance in front, air holes at regular intervals around the perimeter, and an elevated entrance in the rear. They are all about the same size, and all were charcoal kilns. Moreover, if the Cochran kilns had been smelters, there would be slag at their bases, and there is none.

Disputes about who built them and when are beside the point. The kilns at Cochran have an almost otherworldly appearance as they stand across the Gila from Cochran, with the verdant foliage along the river in the foreground and the reddish-brown cliffs of North Butte rising behind them.

Enjoy the beauty of the Cochran kilns through binoculars or a telescope. They are on private property which is posted "No Trespassing." If you want to see and touch a kiln, visit the Walker site near Prescott. You can reach that structure easily (see p. 23).

WHEN YOU GO: From Florence, take Butte Avenue, which becomes the Florence-Kelvin Highway, east for about 17 miles. Drive north on Cochran Road for 12 miles. The kilns will come into view off to the west before you reach the railroad tracks that mark the site of Cochran. A high-clearance vehicle is required. This is a fair-weather trip only, as you will cross and drive along hundreds of yards of normally dry washes.

One of the "must sees" for ghost town enthusiasts is this view of five charcoal kilns built about 1882 along the Gila River. The area is now on private property. This photograph was taken from the vanished town of Cochran.
PHILIP VARNEY

CHAPTER 6

Ghosts of Silverbell

As the main pathway through the southern Arizona Territory, the Gila Trail played an important role in the development of the West. Reincarnated today as Interstates 8 and 10, the trail was cut as a wagon road through the desert wilderness by the Mormon Battalion in 1846. It was traveled by California-bound gold seekers three years later and by the Butterfield stage line in 1858.

On April 15, 1862, Union and Confederate forces met along the Gila Trail at Picacho Pass. The resulting skirmish, which left three soldiers dead and five wounded, would go down in history as the westernmost fatal conflict of the Civil War.

Beginning in 1864, the Gila Trail became the crucial supply route between the Yuma Quartermaster Depot (see p. 53) and forts in southern Arizona, New Mexico, and western Texas. Supplies from Yuma ensured the safe settlement of the Arizona Territory. In 1880, the Southern Pacific Railroad paralleled much of the Gila Trail as it crossed Arizona.

Three of the ghost towns in this chapter are on a loop drive just a few miles west of the historic Gila Trail. Readily accessible from both Tucson and Phoenix, the loop includes Silverbell, a copper mining settlement that was born in the 1860s and died in the 1920s. A later company town, spelled "Silver Bell," occupied a site a few miles from the original camp from 1948 until the 1980s.

In ghost-hunting parlance, both Silverbells are examples of a "place where." While some people require

(Above) *The first Silverbell boasted 3,000 residents at its peak. This 1905 photo shows the mill and period homes. The mine produced copper until 1921.*
JEREMY ROWE COLLECTION
(Facing Page) *From a prominence near the cemetery, through a telephoto lens, one can see what little remains of old Silverbell.*
JOHN DREW

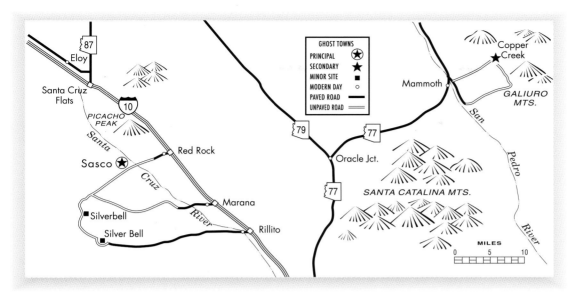

standing buildings and headframes to find visiting a site worthwhile, others take pleasure just standing in an area that once exploded with activity, even if little evidence of that activity remains.

Also along the loop is Sasco, an acronym for the Southern Arizona Smelting Company. Built in 1907, Sasco served as the smelter town for the mines at Silverbell and nearby Picacho Peak. Of the three ghost towns on this loop, Sasco's remains are the most visible.

I began searching out ghost towns in the early 1970s as a way to find new out-of-the-way places, to have a destination rather than just to meander haphazardly. Copper Creek, a remote mining camp dating from the 1880s, is one of my favorite finds. It is located in a beautiful, often overlooked mountain range: the Galiuros. There is enough evidence of mining to get a sense of the people who lived and worked there, and a short but exhilarating hike reveals one of the Arizona backcountry's most startling sites: the Mansion on Copper Creek.

Silverbell, Silver Bell, and Sasco Loop

Silverbell has been twice a ghost. The more recent of the two "Bells" was located near the end of the pavement on Avra Valley Road. Huge tailings dumps and ponds are ample indication of the copper mine that was in production from 1948 into the 1980s. Yet only scant evidence of the company town remains, and what remains has been completely obscured: The road that formerly merely skirted the town has been rerouted well south of the townsite so that you cannot see Silver Bell at all.

When I visited Silver Bell on a bicycle trip in the early 1980s, I talked with a woman who had lived in the well-planned, well-groomed community since its cre-

ation. We stood in her front yard and looked across Aguirre Valley to the distant Baboquivari and Kitt peaks, then back to her town. About half of its buildings were already removed. She spoke sadly of having to leave her closely knit town to move to the expanding metropolis of Tucson.

The original Silverbell (one word), stood north of the newer community. Just before Avra Valley Road enters private property near the location of the newer Silver

(Above) *Some Arizona mining towns of long ago were determined to make their community names last forever. Sasco residents cast theirs in concrete.*
Philip Varney
(Facing Page) *At dawn the smelter ruins at Sasco have the aura of Old World catacombs.*
John Drew

Bell, Silverbell Road takes off to the west, heading toward the older Silverbell. En route are the contrasting sights of enormous tailings dumps, marvelous stands of saguaro, a volcanic-looking slag dump from an old smelter, and expansive vistas.

At about the 6.8-mile point, a lesser road with a locked gate heads east. Survey the shallow valley and hills in front of you. This is all that's left of the original Silverbell, and that road used to be the public route into the townsite.

Remarkably, Silverbell was home to an estimated 3,000 residents from the 1860s into the 1920s. The town's boom began in 1902 when E.B. Gage and W.F. Staunton, along with the Development Company of America, consolidated claims in the mining district into the Imperial Copper Company. A post office was estab-

Grave markers sag with age in the Silverbell Cemetery northwest of Tucson.
JOHN DREW

lished in 1904, and a Wells Fargo station opened in 1906. Prosperity lasted until 1911 when a shaft fire and financial problems led the company to file for bankruptcy. The American Smelting and Refining Company ran operations here from 1915 until 1921, when low prices made mining this grade of copper ore unprofitable.

Beyond that locked turnoff .6 of a mile on the main road is the most enduring reminder of this once-thriving mining town: its cemetery. Several weathered crosses and the grave of Mary O'Toole are reached by walking 400 feet along a sandy track west of the road. A second, smaller section of the cemetery is 250 feet farther down the trail. Here a "cradle fence" protects the grave of an unidentified infant.

The 12-mile stretch between Silverbell and Sasco is an interesting drive, particularly for railroad buffs. Much of the route is on the right-of-way of the Arizona Southern Railroad, built in 1904 to carry ore from the mills at Silverbell to the smelter at Sasco. The tracks were taken up in 1934. Sections of the present road that are inordinately flat, wide, and smooth were the railroad bed. Where a trestle or bridge once spanned a wash, the road is no longer a dirt highway but a normal desert back road.

Sasco was once a community of about 600, which featured a smelter, associated company buildings, residences, saloons, stores, and the Hotel Rockland. A post office served the community from 1907 until 1919. Today remnants of Sasco are scattered over a wide area.

A minor dirt road heading south about .1 of a mile east of a large power line leads to a concrete powder house, foundations of two adobe buildings, and a waterless stone fountain.

East of that turnoff, a road to the north off the main road goes to the ruins of the smelter. An exploration on foot leads to the old smelter stack base (inscribed "Sasco, '07"), the smelter foundations, a series of concrete monoliths, an enormous slag pile, and a railroad platform with the name of the town etched in concrete. East of the main site stands a structure that says "City Hall" but that actually was a jail. Beyond it stand the volcanic stone walls of the Hotel Rockland, vandalized, spray- painted, and forlorn.

A short drive east to La Osa Ranch Road, then north

.6 of a mile to a "Y" in the road, leads to the Sasco Cemetery. Among the memorials are several concrete crosses, reminders of the devastating influenza epidemic of 1918-1919 that claimed more than a half-million American victims.

(Above) *The crumbling walls of Sasco's Rockland Hotel rest near the right-of-way of the old Arizona Southern Railroad.*
JOHN DREW
(Right) *Many Arizona pioneers gambled big money on mines in the territory, accumulating countless stock certificates. Often they proved worthless, but this certificate issued by the Consolidated Copper Creek Mining Co. in 1908 was a winner.*
ARIZONA MINING AND MINERAL MUSEUM

From here it's about a 7-mile journey to Red Rock and I-10, much of it beside irrigation ditches and cattle pens. The Arizona Southern Railroad followed the same route to its connecting point with the Southern Pacific Railroad.

WHEN YOU GO: Begin the loop at Exit 242 (Avra Valley Road) off Interstate 10 (about 16 miles north of downtown Tucson). Drive west 23 miles to the Silver Bell Mine. A high-clearance vehicle is required.

Copper Creek

Mining began along Copper Creek in 1863 with the Yellow Bird claim, but real digging didn't begin until the 1880s. While the veins originally showed silver and lead, copper eventually became the dominant mineral. People were transported to and from the area by the Copper Creek Stage Line. A resident physician served the estimated 200 residents who lived in the community's 50 buildings. Houses dotted the hillsides and were clustered along the creek, with most homes having just one bedroom and a combination living room-kitchen. The principal operations, in what was known as the Bunker Hill Mining District, were those of Copper Creek Mining, Calumet and Arizona, and Minnesota Arizona Mining.

Roy Sibley came to Copper Creek around the turn of the century as manager of the Minnesota Arizona Mining Company, which eventually bought out the Copper Creek claims.

His wife, Belle, served as the first postmaster in 1907.

The Sibleys were determined to bring culture and refinement to the copper camp, at least where their lodgings were concerned. In 1908 they began constructing a 20-room stone mansion, reportedly using Indian labor. The home featured a second-story balcony, polished oak floors, full-length mirrors, and picture windows. Fruit trees grew on the patio. The Sibleys entertained investors at their glorious home, no doubt impressing them with the obvious financial advantages of putting capital into Copper Creek mines.

The Sibleys didn't live in their mansion long, apparently leaving the area around 1910. Martin E. Tew, a partner in the mining company, reorganized the firm as the Copper State Mining Company, but all mines were closed by 1917. By the end of World War I, the Sibley Mansion had been stripped of all valuables. Martin Tew remained in the area, turning the property into the Monte Bonito Ranch. A poet and nature lover, Tew posted verses on trees for visitors to read and left notices requesting that birds and animals be left undisturbed.

One such poem, written in 1936, reveals Tew's love of the land. The last two verses of "A Welcome Pilgrim," which tells of a person in true harmony with nature, read:

He saw the evening come with silent tread
To place upon this majesty his robe
Of royal purple, while the setting sun
Gave every peak a jeweled crown of gold.

Abundantly he took of this vast wealth,
Then freely gave to those who could receive,
Making himself more rich with every gift.
How welcome was the pilgrim to our gates,
Who knew and spoke the language of the gods.

In 1933 the Arizona Molybdenum Corporation reopened the Copper Creek operations. During that time the *San Diego Union* described Copper Creek as a wild, lawless place. An irate citizen complained to the newspaper that the town never had a saloon and that, "...excepting the ore mills, the school house is the largest building, and the teachers rank with the best." Operations had ceased by the time the post office closed in 1942.

Copper Creek Road heads east into the Galiuros. To reach it take State Route 77 to Mammoth. Just north of Mammoth, the highway crosses the San Pedro River. Just north of that bridge River Road heads south. Take that road 2.2 miles to a dirt road heading east. This is Copper Creek Road, which will go through a sandy wash, abruptly climb up a ridge, and begin an obvious ascent into the Galiuros.

Once on the ridge, Copper Creek Road is friendly for about 6 miles, then dives into the canyon as it passes an empty spot on the right that was the ranch once owned by "Sister" Eulalia Bourne, a rancher, schoolteacher, and author of several books, including the memoir *Woman in Levis*. From this point the road deteriorates markedly, crossing and recrossing the creek and hugging the canyon walls. (*Warning*: Do not attempt to cross Copper Creek if it is running swiftly.)

Once there, 8 miles from the beginning of Copper Creek Road, you will begin to see ample evidence of mining, with tailings dumps, chutes, a bridge, and a narrow-gauge railroad bed. As you leave the creek, a short, steep climb takes you to the site of the old store

and post office. There, set in rock, stands a deteriorating concrete sign bearing the name of the community.

The road to the right goes to the Bunker Hill Mine. To reach the trail to the Sibley Mansion, go to the left. This fork takes you back down to the creek near a large concrete dam. Cross the creek and follow the road as it doubles back upstream a quarter mile or so. Leave your vehicle and hike upstream along the once-passable road that follows Copper Creek, with its lovely ash and sycamore honor guard, for 45 minutes (about 1.5 miles). Along the way you'll see a large two-cylinder diesel engine that once powered a tramway up the mountainside and, farther on, a couple of roofless ruins.

Eventually you will come upon the stunning stone ruins of the Mansion on Copper Creek standing in a majestic grove of sycamore, ash, and oak. A few hundred yards beyond, on the opposite bank, stands a stone building that was once a store and offices.

In 1992 a Tucson newspaper extolled the beauty of the Copper Creek area, bringing a horde of people who left behind trash and trampled flora. Please be considerate of the people who live in and love this wonderful area.

WHEN YOU GO: Start at Mammoth, about 45 miles from downtown Tucson on State Route 77. Copper Creek is located approximately 12 miles east of Mammoth. The Sibley mansion is a couple more miles' walk upstream. A four-wheel-drive, high-clearance vehicle is necessary.

CHAPTER 7

Santa Cruz Ghosts

The Santa Cruz Trail, which roughly follows the river of the same name, was first used by prehistoric Indians as a trade route. Spaniards traveled it as early as the 1500s. In 1691 Father Eusebio Francisco Kino followed the trail to establish a string of missions in the area known as Pimeria (the land of the Pima Indians). To protect the missions and nearby ranches and mines from Indian attack, Spaniards built two fortified outposts, or *presidios*: Tubac in 1752, Tucson in 1775. By 1821, Mexico's revolution had ejected the Spanish, and Mexico took control of the outposts.

At least four of the ghost towns and mining camps in this region date from Spanish and Mexican sovereignty: Tubac, Arivaca, Cerro Colorado, and Salero. With the Gadsden Purchase of 1854, the United States bought southern Arizona from Mexico for $10 million, extending American territory from the Gila River south to the present border. By the late 1850s, Americans were

searching for mineral deposits in the Santa Cruz Valley and reopening earlier Spanish and Mexican diggings.

During the Civil War (1861-1865), U.S. troops that had protected local settlers were reassigned to the war effort. As a result, Indian attacks increased, curtailing mining efforts. The end of the Civil War brought increased security to the area; mining and ranching activity resumed and prospered. Most of the ghost towns and mining camps here date from this later expansion.

This chapter features sites in two areas. First, the Ruby Loop: Highlights include the Heintzelman Mine at Cerro Colorado, site of an infamous murder; Arivaca, a historic ranching and military site; Ruby, one of the most extensive ghost towns in the West; and Tubac, the oldest European settlement in Arizona. Part of the loop is in Pima County, although the historical and financial ties of all the sites are to the towns of Tubac and Nogales in Santa Cruz County.

(Above) *Deputy Sheriff R.Q. Leatherwood, left, and Sheriff Henry Saxon, right, captured (l - r) Placido Silvas and Manuel Martinez, who murdered Ruby storekeeper Frank Phearson and his wife in 1921. Silvas later escaped and was never brought to justice.*
Arizona Historical Society
(Facing Page) *The ghost town of Ruby in Santa Cruz County sleeps peacefully today, but it had a violent and bloody past.*
John Drew

The second area is the Patagonia-Sonoita Loop, with five ghost towns between Patagonia and the Mexican border: Harshaw, with a small hillside cemetery; Mowry, site of a silver mine confiscated during the Civil War; Washington Camp and Duquesne, sister towns with revitalized buildings and decaying remnants; and Lochiel, a former border crossing where foundations and a charming one-room school await. Then the road traverses the picturesque San Rafael Valley, locale for the film *Oklahoma!*, and proceeds to the ghost of Sunnyside.

In addition to these two main loops, each trip offers extensions for true back-roads explorers.

The Ruby Loop

Cerro Colorado, the town, was named for a small red mound just south of the Cerro Colorado ("red hill" in Spanish) Mountains. It was the site of one of the best-known mining efforts of the 1850s, the Heintzelman Mine. From Arivaca Junction off Interstate 19, take the Arivaca road southwest about 14 miles. Turn right at the

Circle 46 Ranch's prominent mailbox and wrought-iron sign. The ranch road heads almost directly west from the Arivaca Road. After .2 of a mile on the ranch road, there stands a concrete casketlike grave said to be that of John Poston.

Charles D. Poston, called the "Father of Arizona," organized the Sonora Exploring and Mining Company in 1855 with headquarters in Tubac. Samuel Colt, the gun maker whose name is forever linked with the West, invested in the company. The company's president was Samuel P. Heintzelman, a West Point graduate who had established the post at Fort Yuma (see p. 53) in 1850.

The silver mine — actually it was a reworking of Spanish and Mexican efforts — became the company's biggest producer, but also a source of tragedy. For a while the mine's diggings met with considerable success. Then Apache attacks and a collapsed-shaft accident that killed 15 miners caused worker unrest. And finally, recurring rumors of a buried cache of silver led to murder. In 1861 John Poston, left in charge of the mine by his brother Charles, and two German employees were found slain.

John Poston, the brother of Charles D. Poston, the man known as the "Father of Arizona," is buried in this concrete vault at the Cerro Colorado Mine. He was murdered at the site in 1861.
PHILIP VARNEY

This police wagon dates back six decades. It now rusts away beneath the brush at Las Guijas.
PHILIP VARNEY

Seven bandits from Mexico, believed to have been looking for the buried silver, were the suspected culprits. This violent act marked the beginning of the end at the Cerro Colorado Mine.

When J. Ross Browne passed through the area of the Heintzelman Mine in the mid-1860s, he wrote in his journal, "At the time of our visit it was silent and desolate — a picture of utter abandonment . . . . Nothing was to be seen but wreck and ruin, and the few solitary graves on a neighboring hill, which tell the story of violence and sacrifice by which the pathway to civilization has been marked in Arizona."

Today little evidence remains except John Poston's grave. The foundations of a mill, its tailings pond, and a headframe across a draw at an occupied residence all date from later mining attempts.

(*Historical note*: The resting place of John Poston's brother Charles, one of Arizona's most influential pioneers, is located north of Florence on Poston's Butte. The memorial is a rock and concrete pyramid.)

Las Guijas (Spanish for "conglomerate" or "quartz pebbles") lies beyond Cerro Colorado 7.1 miles on the same dirt road (see p. 135 for specific directions). It was a gold mine named for the rock in which the ore was found in the 1860s. This site is strictly for the "purist." There is little evidence other than diggings on the hillside to the south and a series of foundations just as the road takes a right. The most interesting thing here, however, had nothing to do with the mine. Down in a wash beyond the first foundation are tailings that look like fine sand. Up under some brush, trapped in the sand, stands an old paddy wagon from the 1930s or '40s!

Arivaca is a delightful community of about 150 people that is neither a ghost town nor a mining camp but is well worth a visit. Originally settled by Pima and Tohono O'odham (Papago) Indians, the town received its name

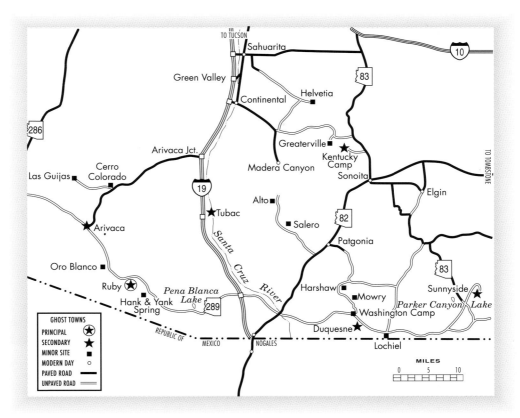

from a Spanish ranch called La Aribac, which was abandoned in 1751. In 1812 Tomas and Ignacio Ortiz purchased the ranch from the Spanish colonial government. Charles Poston and his Sonora Exploring and Mining Company bought it from the Ortiz family in 1856 for a reported $10,000.

Mining has long ceased to be important to Arivaca, but ranching remains. The town had one other life, as an Army outpost guarding against border incursions encouraged by Kaiser Wilhelm. To divert American attention from Europe during World War I, the Kaiser tried in vain to get Mexico to attack the United States. An important officer stationed at the outpost was Gen. John "Black Jack" Pershing, so-called because he commanded African-American troopers.

Evidence of that Army post is a private two-building adobe home on the south side of the street. It was built in the 1880s and used later as the military doctor's residence and clinic. Across the street stands the Arivaca Mercantile, built in 1912 but destroyed by fire in 1956 and rebuilt the same year.

West of the mercantile and across the street beyond a restaurant-bar are the adobe ruins of what some claim was Teresa Celaya's house. It was supposedly to this house that her brothers fled after robbing the Vulture Mine (see p. 24) of two gold bricks, which legend says stand. Because the area was so close to the Mexican bor-der and raids in the area were all too common, Clarke and his wife, Gypsy, kept firearms in every room of their house and store. Their son, Dan, a popular lifelong Arizonan who died in 1992, confided to me that his father sent his mother to California to give birth, because conditions in Ruby were too dangerous. Dan always was a bit chagrined that he wasn't actually born in Arizona.

On one occasion, the lives of the Clarke family may have been saved by a tall tale. During a time when all ranchers and miners were concerned about cross-border raids by Mexican revo-lutionaries, Clarke was asked by an old man named Guzman what the new pipe apparatus was in front of his store. Clarke loved to kid the serious old man, so he told him that it was an elaborate device by which he could release a spray of poi-son gas with a master switch in his bed-room. He said it was strong enough to wipe out a regiment. Clarke enjoyed a good laugh as the old man made a wide detour around the cylinder. In truth, the device was nothing but a rain gauge!

When Guzman returned about a month later, Clarke asked him if he had encoun-tered any revolutionary soldiers. "Oh, yes . . . They went through everything I had. But they took only my tobacco." Clarke then asked if the soldiers had considered coming to the Ruby store. Guzman replied, "Yes, they asked me all about it and I told them about that thing you have there — that thing that shoots poison gas." The soldiers decided to avoid the Ruby store. From then on, Clarke said, "I was very careful to tell everyone about my 'death-dealing machine.'"

Others were not as lucky. Clarke leased the store to Alex and John Frasier in 1920, warning them to keep well armed, especially when behind the counter. Less than two months later, Alex lay dead by the cash register and John, shot in the eye after being forced to open the store safe, lived only a few hours longer. One of the two bandits was later killed resisting arrest, but not before killing a deputy. The other was never apprehended.

Clarke was still feeling guilty about the situation into which he had put the Frasier brothers when Frank Phearson approached him about purchasing the store. Phearson brushed words of caution aside, arguing that lawlessness had decreased sufficiently and that another attack was highly unlikely. Phearson became the store's next owner, and on August 26, 1921, he and his wife were killed by seven armed men. Their young daughter, Margaret, fell while trying to escape; she looked up to see

(Top) *The doctor's office and hospital stood close to the mining operations at Ruby.*
(Above) *Ruby, named for the first postmaster's wife, is known as one of the West's premier ghost towns. The store, left, and jail are two surviving buildings.*
(Facing Page, Top) *This panorama of Ruby confirms that the town has more standing buildings than any other Arizona ghost town except Vulture.*
(Facing Page, Bottom) *Ruby's schoolhouse once echoed with the clamor of students in eight grades.*
ALL BY PHILIP VARNEY

her pursuer stop over her and then, unaccountably, turn and walk back inside the store. Margaret Phearson Anderson, her life spared for whatever reason, lived to become a teacher and reading specialist in Nogales and Tucson, retiring in 1980.

Two of the seven bandits were recognized as they fled Ruby. Placido Silvas and Manuel Martinez were taken into custody, tried, convicted, and sentenced to hang. The sheriff's car transporting them to Florence overturned, killing the sheriff and injuring his deputy. Martinez was later recaptured and hanged at the Florence prison. Silvas was never found; it is conceivable, although highly unlikely, that he is still alive today.

The most prosperous period for Ruby began in 1926 when the Eagle-Picher Lead Company took over operations. The town boasted electricity (supplied by diesel engines), a doctor, a hospital, and a school with eight grades and three teachers. From 1934 to 1937, the Montana Mine was the leading producer of lead and zinc in Arizona. In 1936 it was third in silver production. But the ore played out in 1940, and by 1941 the town that once claimed 2,000 residents became a ghost.

Today Ruby has more than two dozen buildings under roof. The Clarke store, which was habitable until the 1970s, has completely collapsed, but the sturdy jail next

door remains. The school stands nearby, with its basketball backboards dangling in place and two toppled teacherages adjacent to the playground.

On the southern side of the townsite are mine offices, mill foundations, mine officials' residences, and a single-miners' dormitory. Several of the southern buildings are visible from the road or atop a small hill.

Hank and Yank Spring is reached by a dirt road that cuts off from the Ruby Road in Bear Valley, 5 miles east of Ruby at the sign to Sycamore Canyon. The track proceeds for about .1 of a mile to a parking area. From there, it's about a five-minute walk to an adobe wall, all that remains of the ranching efforts of Hank Hewitt and John "Yank" Bartlett.

In April of 1886 the ranch was attacked by Apache warriors who fatally wounded visiting neighbor Phil Shanahan. Ten-year-old Johnny Bartlett managed to slip out of the ranch and run about 9 miles to old Oro Blanco for help. The 13 men who responded to the call found the Apaches had disappeared, taking with them about 50 horses. But the courage of Johnny Bartlett was not forgotten. Dubbed "The Hero of the Bear Valley Raid," Johnny was presented with an inscribed rifle by the territorial government.

The final 8 miles of Ruby Road traverse some of the most beautiful backroads ranching country in Arizona, ending at the pavement at Peña Blanca ("white rock") Lake. Interstate 19 is 10 miles farther east.

The planned community of Rio Rico is north of the Ruby Road on I-19. This was once the site of Calabasas, where the now-vanished Santa Rita Hotel was reputed to have the finest lodgings between El Paso and San Diego.

Farther north are the ruins of the Tumacacori Mission, which was built in the late 1700s and has been a national monument since 1908. Less than 4 miles beyond the mission stands the town of Tubac.

(**Above**) *Until 1886 when Geronimo surrendered, hostile Apaches made mining in southern Arizona a risky business. These well-armed warriors, led by Natches, harassed early settlers in the territory.*
ARIZONA STATE LIBRARY, ARCHIVES AND PUBLIC RECORDS
(**Facing Page**) *James Finley purchased the major mining claim at Harshaw in 1887. His family home was this once-elegant brick residence.*
PHILIP VARNEY

Tubac, founded in 1752, is the oldest European settlement in Arizona. In addition to serving as headquarters for Charles Poston's Sonora Exploring and Mining Company, the presidio was also the site of Arizona's first newspaper, *The Weekly Arizonian,* which debuted in 1859. It was this newspaper that caused Arizona's first recorded duel. Sylvester Mowry, a prominent mine owner (see Mowry, p. 110) was criticized by *Arizonian* editor Edward Cross for supporting efforts to make Arizona a territory separate from New Mexico. Mowry challenged Cross to a duel with rifles. When neither was able to inflict so much as a wound, the two concluded their confrontation by toasting each other's health (and probably their poor marksmanship).

Visitors to Tubac should stop at the state park museum, which gives insight into life along the Santa Cruz Trail. Other attractions include the 1885 Old Tubac School, St. Anne's Church, and the Tubac Cemetery just north of the main plaza on Burruel Street.

WHEN YOU GO: Drive south from Tucson on I-19 to Exit 48, Arivaca Junction and Amado. Turn right off the interstate to Arivaca Junction, then west on Arivaca Road. A high-clearance vehicle is recommended beyond Arivaca. If you wish to visit Las Guijas or Hank and Yank Spring, a high-clearance vehicle is required.

The Patagonia - Sonoita Loop

The ghost towns south of Patagonia and Sonoita have just enough remnants to remind the visitor that this was once a place of frantic exploration, abundant greed, and frequent violence. And, in the case of one community, a place of religious tolerance and brotherhood.

Patagonia, 18 miles northeast of Nogales, is one of Arizona's most charming small towns. Its centerpiece is a turn-of-the-century depot that was constructed for the New Mexico and Arizona Railroad, which in 1881-1882 connected Nogales to the Southern Pacific main line at Benson. The track was abandoned in 1962, but the depot was saved by the efforts of local citizens. On back streets, several adobe buildings remain from days when Patagonia was the connecting point between nearby mines and the rest of the world. On one hill is a picturesque school; a sizable cemetery is located on another hill southwest of town near the highway to Nogales.

Incidentally, the best day to visit Patagonia is the Fourth of July, when an old-fashioned parade wends through town.

Harshaw, the first of the ghost towns on this loop, lies 8 miles southeast of Patagonia. In Patagonia, turn south off State Route 82 onto Taylor Avenue. Then turn east after one block onto Harshaw Avenue and continue for about 6 miles, where the road intersects with unpaved FR 49 and a sign directs you to the townsite.

Rancher David Tecumseh Harshaw should have thanked Tom Jeffords (see Fort Bowie, p. 126) for making him a rich man. When Harshaw was grazing cattle on Apache land in 1877, Indian Agent Jeffords ordered him to remove them. Harshaw relocated his herd to this area and discovered a tremendously rich silver vein, which he named the Hermosa. Within two years Harshaw, who named the mining town that rose near the mine after himself, had sold his holdings to a New York concern and moved on.

The Hermosa Mine, located due south of Harshaw up a Jeep trail, became the major producer in the area (peaking at a reported $365,654 during a four-month period in 1880). The population of Harshaw reached an estimated 2,000. The town's life span, however, was very short. A violent thunderstorm, a fire, and a drop in ore quality led to its demise. An 1882 article in the *Tombstone Epitaph* told of a place where 80 percent of the more than 200 buildings were unoccupied, with " . . . windows smashed and doors standing open." This is the same Harshaw that only two years earlier had its own newspaper, the *Arizona Bullion*, and a bustling mile-long main street with a reported seven saloons.

Harshaw had two minor rebirths. One began in 1887 when Tucsonan James Finley purchased the Hermosa claim for $600. This time the mining lasted longer but on a much smaller scale, and only about 100 residents lived in the town. In 1903 Finley died, the market price of silver dropped significantly, and by 1909 the town was a ghost once again.

The community of Harshaw last saw limited life from 1937 until 1956 as the Arizona Smelting and Refining Company (ASARCO) worked the nearby Flux and Trench mines.

A tin-roofed adobe residence marks the intersection of FR 49 and the private, side road that heads east into what is left of the Harshaw community. Down that private road about 200 yards stands the site's primary remnant, the once-elegant brick residence of James Finley.

The wooden porch, with its graceful, curving tin roof, and the skillful brickwork make the Finley home one of Arizona's most architecturally pleasing historic buildings.

A small, interesting cemetery is situated on a hillside west of FR 49, the road from Patagonia, across cottonwood-lined Harshaw Creek. Some of the headstones and wrought iron markers date from the 1880s.

One particularly poignant marker reads:

"Freddie Lee Sorrells. Born February 14, 1880. Died June 5, 1885. A little time on earth he spent, till God for him an angel sent."

Mowry is just under 5 miles south of Harshaw on FR 49. Turn east on FR 214 and proceed .2 of mile to the townsite. Mowry is one of the oldest mining camps in Arizona. Originally called the Patagonia Mine, it was worked by Mexicans in 1857 and perhaps even earlier by Spanish Jesuit priests. Sylvester Mowry, a West Point graduate stationed at Fort Crittenden, purchased the mine in 1859 for $20,000. Renamed Mowry Mine, it became an enormous success, with 12 blast furnaces reducing the rich ore into 70-pound bars. The total amount shipped was a reported $1.5 million. It was also in 1859 that Mowry had his duel with newspaperman Edward Cross (see p. 109). Mowry was passionate about Arizona controlling its destiny by separating from New Mexico. As he wrote in 1864, "The history of Arizona has had two aspects — one of great and steady improvement, the other of calamity and decline. The first was the result of the great natural resources of the Territory; the second . . . the shameful abandonment and neglect of the country by the administration at Washington."

The Civil War completely reversed Sylvester Mowry's fortunes. He was arrested in 1862, charged with treason for selling lead for Confederate bullets, sent to prison at Fort Yuma, and had his mine confiscated. As he himself put it, "In June 1862, the proprietor of the Mowry Silver Mines was seized by a large armed force, under the orders of Gen. J.H. Carleton, while in the legitimate pursuit of his business, and retained as a political prisoner for six months. This seizure was made upon a false, ridiculous, and malicious charge. After nearly six months close imprisonment the

(Above) *Harshaw and its mine, located 8 miles southeast of Patagonia, date back to the 1870s. This decaying adobe home is a link with its colorful past.*
PHILIP VARNEY
(Right) *Harshaw was born in 1877 when rancher David Harshaw discovered silver on his range. It was a bustling community in the 1880s, when this photo was taken.*
ARIZONA HISTORICAL SOCIETY

writer was discharged, 'there being no evidence' [in the opinion of the court that tried his case], 'either oral or documentary against him;' a charming commentary upon the constitutional guarantee to every citizen of 'life, liberty, and the pursuit of happiness.'"

Despite Mowry's release and eventual exoneration, he never did get his mine back. The property was auctioned, and the winning bid was a mere $4,000 — paid by the auctioneer, Marshal Cutler. According to Mowry, the mine was clearing more than that *per week* during peak production. Whether Mowry ever received compensation for the injustice done to him is a matter of dispute. He died in England in 1871 at the age of 39. The mine never had any significant production after the Civil War.

At Mowry today stand a crumbling adobe wall on one side of FR 214 and a small stone foundation on the other. Up a road to the north stand more adobe walls. Beyond the walls are the mine and smelter site, with a collapsed shaft, stone powder house, and large smelter slag pile.

Washington Camp is slightly more than 4 miles south of Mowry, just south of the junction of FR 49 and Duquesne Road (FR 61). The largest community south of Patagonia, it shows little evidence of its antiquity. The area was prospected in the early 1860s but abandoned because of recurring Apache attacks. Boom years began in the late 1880s when Duquesne Mining and Reduction Company of Pittsburgh purchased claims and began operations at what became the town of Duquesne (doo-*kane*). Besides the mine, Duquesne had company offices and mining officials' residences. Washington Camp had the reduction plant, miners' bunkhouses, a general store, and a school. Eventually each camp contained about 1,000 residents. "The two camps was so close together," one resident claimed, "people used to say that when Duquesne's tail was stepped on, it was Washington that barked!"

Duquesne offers more rewarding ghost town remnants than Washington Camp. Four-tenths of a mile past Washington Camp, take FR 128, a rough road branching to the right from FR 61 (a high-clearance vehicle is recommended). Still standing are several buildings as well as evidence of the mine itself. The most interesting structure is a once-stately house with a large porch partly obscured by trees and brush that is across a draw to the west. The house is on private property, and it is posted against trespassing.

Continue through Duquesne on FR 128 until it returns to FR 61. From there it's almost 4 miles south to a monument to Fray Marcos de Niza, vice commissary of the Franciscan Order and delegate of the viceroy in Mexico, who is said to have passed through this vicinity in 1539. The monument commemorates him as the first European to enter the United States west of the Rockies.

Lochiel, on FR 61 southeast of the monument, was a crossing point into Mexico until the early 1980s, when it was closed for budgetary reasons. The vicinity's first post office, opened in 1880, was for a place called Luttrell, apparently named for Dr. J.M. Luttrell, who ran a boardinghouse and owned the Holland Company Smelting Works. Another post office opened two years later as *La Noria* (Spanish for "a well-water lifting device"), apparently within a mile of Luttrell. Both closed in 1883.

In 1884 another post office opened, this time as Lochiel, named by ranchers Colin and Brewster Cameron for their ancestral home in Scotland. Although "La Noria" appears as a post office again in 1909, "Lochiel" has stuck. By whatever name, the community once featured two smelters for neighboring mines, the usual saloons, a butcher shop, and an estimated population of

(Above) *The mining company headquarters at Duquesne is posted against trespassing, but you can get a good view from the road through town.*
PHILIP VARNEY

400. Mexican revolutionary Pancho Villa and his men often came across the border in this area, stealing cattle before returning to the safety of Mexico.

Today Lochiel sits among the cottonwoods, a delightful escape from urban life. The cemetery rests on a hilltop overlooking a church and the old U. S. Customs station, all now on private property. An adobe one-room schoolhouse, built in 1918, stands adjacent to its teacherage. In the 1980s the town had a school board, a budget, and applications from teachers interested in the challenge of a one-room school. The school at Lochiel had everything — except a single student.

Lochiel is nestled in the corner of the San Rafael Valley, one of southern Arizona's most scenic places. Hollywood came to this lush valley to film *Monte Walsh*, *Oklahoma!*, and *Tom Horn*. Turning the San Rafael Valley, at an altitude of more than 5,000 feet, into rural Oklahoma was an expensive proposition. Ten acres of corn had to be coddled, watered, and nurtured with chemicals. One wag at the time estimated the cost to be about $8.95 per ear. The film crew also carefully hung 2,000 wax peaches on nonbearing peach trees every morning and took them in at night. Ah, Hollywood.

Sunnyside is 20 miles east of Lochiel or 32 miles south of Sonoita (for specific directions, see p. 135). After turning off the Sunnyside Road (FR 227) onto FR 228, you'll find the last 3.2 miles to the townsite require a high-clearance vehicle.

Sunnyside is unusual among Arizona's ghost towns because it had no saloons, no brothels — not even a jail. This mining town was also a religious community.

Samuel Donnelly, a frequent patron of bars in San Francisco in the 1880s, changed his ways and became a Salvation Army preacher. Brother Donnelly brought a group of followers from Tombstone to work the Lone Star and Copper Glance mines and to create a community based on brotherhood and Christian fellowship.

Families lived in separate quarters but had their meals in a communal building. People contributed to the group according to their talents, such as working at the mine or in the prosperous sawmill, teaching school, or giving music lessons. Sunnyside was known for its generosity to passersby and even gave scholarship money to the University of Arizona.

Samuel Donnelly died in 1901, but the community survived for many more years. In 1932 the mine closed and the townsite was sold.

I first visited Sunnyside in 1975 and have returned

countless times. In addition to the buildings (schoolhouse, two family residences, sawmill, and Brother Donnelly's unpretentious cabin) and the beautiful location, I was drawn by the spirit of the place, a spirit embodied by the caretakers at the time, John and Anna McIntyre. They were kind, gracious, and offered a touchstone to the past. John McIntyre came to Sunnyside in 1893 when he was three years old, and had attended, at the turn of the century, the one-room schoolhouse now in ruins at the townsite. The McIntyres died in the late 1980s, and with them went a wonderful piece of Arizona history.

Sunnyside is on private property. Vandalism of the site in recent years has forced the owner to post "No Trespassing" signs around the property to protect this truly unique historic treasure.

WHEN YOU GO: During good weather, when creeks are low, a passenger car can reach Harshaw, Mowry, Washington Camp, and Lochiel. A high-clearance vehicle is required for the roads to Duquesne and Sunnyside.

Additional Sites

Salero ("saltcellar" in Spanish) is an unusual name for a town, and here is one version of how it got its name: "The Bishop of Sonora is coming to visit our Tumacacori mission! This is an event to prepare for: the chapel looking its best, rooms cleaned, special linens for the bed. The bishop is a known connoisseur of food and drink. Have the freshest poultry, the tenderest beef prepared. Be certain the best tableware is ready. But something special should mark the occasion. We will have an elegant saltcellar, fashioned from the silver of our mine, ready near his plate."

Salero, a mine in the Santa Rita Mountains, dates from sometime after the arrival of Spanish Jesuits in the 1690s. A partnership of six men created the Salero Mining Company of Cincinnati, Ohio, and purchased the mine in 1857.

Salero became a steady producer, but not without a price that was typical of the times. All but one of the original partners were victims of Apache attacks. In fact, the two tallest peaks of the Santa Ritas are named after slain officials John Wrightson and Gilbert Hopkins.

By 1865, the Salero Mining Company was defunct. A

(Above) *This may be the last photo taken of the Sunnyside schoolhouse, which collapsed in early 1993.*
(Left) *Sunnyside, 32 miles south of Sonoita, is a jewel of a ghost town that was a religious commune in the 1880s. Its founder was a reformed alcoholic.*
(Right) *Salero (Spanish for "saltcellar") was mined by Spanish priests nearly three centuries ago.*
ALL BY PHILIP VARNEY

113

decade later John E. McGee tried unsuccessfully to resurrect the mine. By the early 1880s the Apache wars were winding down, and from 1884 to 1890 George Clark had the luxury of operating the Salero without the danger of raids.

Today Salero is one of Arizona's better-preserved ghost towns, probably because it has been occupied and therefore protected from vandals. It stands on private property clearly posted against trespassing, but, from a hill to the south, one can get a panoramic view of its four adobe buildings, probably dating from George Clark's ownership.

Alto was the site of another Spanish mine dating from the same period as Salero. Like Salero, it was reopened after the Gadsden Purchase. The Goldtree Mine, named by Joseph Goldtree, was established in 1875 in what was known as the Tyndall Mining District. The original name for the townsite was El Plomo (Spanish for "lead"). At a later, unknown, date the name was changed to Alto ("high"), perhaps because the diggings themselves, still visible from the townsite, are perched on a steep mountainside far above the valley floor.

Only one roofless adobe ruin, the former post office (1907-1933), remains. Alto is worth visiting, however, just for its scenic high-desert surroundings.

WHEN YOU GO: Both sites are on Salero Road, which turns off State Route 82 just under 3 miles southwest of Patagonia. The hill south of the Salero townsite is on the east side of the road 7 miles from the highway. Alto is 4.3 miles beyond Salero on the same road. Under normal, dry conditions, a passenger car can reach Salero, but for the last .7 of a mile to Alto, a high-clearance vehicle, or a willingness to walk, is necessary.

Helvetia has been a copper mining site since before the Civil War, but the main activity did not begin until 1881 with the mining of the Old Dick, Heavyweight, and Tallyho claims of L.M. Grover. In the 1890s the claims were consolidated by the Helvetia Copper Company of New Jersey and the camp came to life with several adobe buildings, saloons, a smelter, and dozens of miners' tents. A post office opened in 1899. Stage service connected the settlement of about 300 to Vail and Tucson.

The price of copper plummeted in 1911, closing the mines. A brief rebirth occurred during World War I, but the post office closed in 1921, effectively sealing the fate of a town that was already dead.

Helvetia is easy to spot at the northwest end of the Santa Rita Mountains because of the chalklike scar in the range due to a later lime quarry. The only remnants of the community are a tiny cemetery, tailings, and the

(Left) *The Forest Service is restoring Kentucky Camp, a town that sprang up at the Kentucky Mine near Sonoita in 1874. This is the company office and boardinghouse.*
(Right) *Helvetia was a copper mine before the Civil War. This building and a cemetery are the lonely reminders of its existence.*
BOTH BY PHILIP VARNEY
(Below) *Helvetia's general store was a busy trading center in 1902. Mining began in this southern Arizona camp before the Civil War, but it did not peak until 1899, when the Helvetia post office was opened.*
ARIZONA HISTORICAL SOCIETY

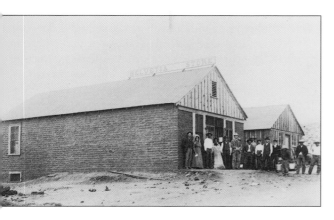

crumbling walls of what once was a large adobe building.

WHEN YOU GO: Helvetia is 15 miles southeast of Sahuarita. See p. 135 for specific directions.

Kentucky Camp is a promising development for ghost town enthusiasts. For many years, in an attempt to return land to its pristine condition, the Forest Service actually leveled buildings, many of which had historic value. Now, in a fortuitous reversal of policy, the same organization is trying to save, preserve, and restore sites on public land. One wonderful example is Kentucky Camp.

The name of the town comes from the Kentucky Mine, which yielded substantial quantities of gold during the excitement at nearby Greaterville in 1874. The gold played out in 1886, and Kentucky Camp was abandoned. It came back to life in 1904 when mining engineer James Stetson believed that he could extract gold from placer deposits by channeling snowmelt runoff from the Santa Rita Mountains and storing it in a reservoir. His plan had the financial backing of Easterner George B. McAneny.

But Stetson died in 1905 from a fall from a third-story window of the Santa Rita Hotel in Tucson (perhaps suicide, although no note was found). The next day he was to address stockholders of McAneny's Santa Rita Mining and Water Company. Shortly thereafter, McAneny died, the water project perished, and Kentucky Camp was abandoned. It was sold for back taxes and became part of a ranch.

The Forest Service acquired Kentucky Camp in 1989 as part of a land swap. Since 1991, "Passport in Time" volunteers, aided by Friends of Kentucky Camp volunteers, have been working to stabilize and in some cases reconstruct the five remaining buildings, one of which can be rented for overnight stays.

Kentucky Camp consists of a combination dormitory-office, an assay office, two residences, and a barn. When I first visited the site in the mid-1980s (with permission of the then-owners), I was impressed at just how well the buildings had survived, probably because of their seclusion, the watchful eye of the owners, and the fact that no ghost town book had mentioned it. The Forest Service and its volunteers are doing a tremendous favor for those of us interested in preserving the history of the West.

WHEN YOU GO: Kentucky Camp is reached taking Gardner Canyon Road and then Fish Canyon Road, which are 7 miles north of Sonoita off State Route 83. The 5-mile route is clearly marked by forest service signs. You will park your vehicle adjacent to a locked gate. It's a few minutes' walk to the townsite. In good weather, a passenger car can make the trip.

CHAPTER 8

Tombstone Territory Ghosts

ochise County, in the southeastern corner of Arizona, remains one of the state's better-kept secrets. Thousands of tourists visit world-famous Tombstone, then leave the territory. Like a prospector looking only for gold, they seek the glitter and bypass many other treasures.

Bisbee is a copper town with more than 90 years of mining history. Because it was the most elegant of Arizona's mining camps, Bisbee has more buildings of architectural significance than any other ghost town featured in this book. Jerome, its only rival, may be more dramatic, hanging off the side of Cleopatra Hill as it does, but Bisbee is more subtle. Tucked into Mule Mountain canyons, Bisbee's back streets evoke a grandeur that even Jerome cannot equal. And, since Bisbee remains the seat of county government, much of the area has been rescued from serious decay.

Cochise County's most famous drawing card is Tombstone, "The Town Too Tough to Die." Other enchanting attractions include the museum at historic Fort Huachuca, at Sierra Vista; the informative Amerind Foundation near Dragoon; the dramatic Chiricahua

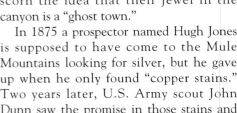

National Monument, southeast of Willcox; the ranch of "Texas" John Slaughter, east of Douglas; and a day-long tour that starts in Tombstone and takes visitors on a back-road journey through Apache country to see an abandoned fort, stagecoach stations, and ghost towns.

Bisbee

Bisbee was the acknowledged "Queen of the Copper Camps." With a peak population of 35,000 and a mining life of almost a century, Bisbee attained a permanence rare among mining towns. Despite fires, floods, labor troubles, and mine shutdowns and rebirths, Bisbee endured. Now, even though the mines have closed, the people of Bisbee scorn the idea that their jewel in the canyon is a "ghost town."

In 1875 a prospector named Hugh Jones is supposed to have come to the Mule Mountains looking for silver, but he gave up when he only found "copper stains." Two years later, U.S. Army scout John Dunn saw the promise in those stains and staked a claim. Since his military obligations precluded his pursuing the veins, he grubstaked George Warren, a

(Above) The Bisbee Massacre of 1883, a bungled bank heist that left five innocent people dead, led to John Heith's unceremonious lynching by citizens irate because Heith had received a mere life sentence for his involvement in the killings.
ARIZONA HISTORICAL SOCIETY
(Facing Page) Tombstone's ornate City Hall, built in 1882, is one of the surviving treasures of the town's colorful past.
PHILIP VARNEY

prospector. Warren apparently shared the information with cronies, so when Dunn finally was able to visit his claims he was dismayed to find miners already working the area, including Warren, who had staked his own claim rather than working Dunn's. The place was already known as the Warren District. Disgusted, Dunn reportedly sold his one stake for $4,000 and left the area.

The man who cheated John Dunn received a kind of justice, however. George Warren later bet his claim on a foot race and lost. That claim was to become known as the Copper Queen, which produced hundreds of millions of dollars' worth of copper ore.

The town that formed near the mines was named Bisbee in honor of San Francisco judge DeWitt Bisbee, an investor who never saw the camp. It was a dangerous place in its early days, with Apache raids still a possibility. As a result, school children had "Indian drills." When they heard the whistle blow two shorts, a long, and a short, they were to scurry to the safety of mine shafts.

By 1878 copper was paying off so well that it was profitable to freight the ore to Benson and send it by rail all the way to Pennsylvania for smelting. Since profits would increase substantially by shipping a finished product, smelting operations began by the next year. Within a few years, the once-forested Mule Mountains were denuded for firewood and the polluting fumes of smelters choked the canyons and gulches where the town developed. Citizens saw dollars in the sulfurous clouds, however, so few complained. Those who could afford it built their homes amidst the cleaner air on the hills above town.

Metallurgist and mining engineer James Douglas had seen some Bisbee ore in a Pennsylvania smelter. In 1881 Douglas came to Bisbee on behalf of Phelps Dodge, a company that had invested in Morenci mines (see p. 84) earlier that year. Phelps Dodge bought into the Copper Queen Mining Company, one of Bisbee's two largest operations. James Douglas became the architect of a mining venture that turned Bisbee from a copper camp into one of the great mining towns of the world.

In 1885 the Copper Queen and its main competition merged into the Copper Queen Consolidated Mining Company, a Phelps Dodge subsidiary. Bisbee reaped the gains of organized management. Copper Queen Consolidated built a company store and a library and enjoyed prosperity that rivaled nearby Tombstone. No one could predict that Tombstone had only one year of affluence left.

Even though Copper Queen Consolidated exerted considerable influence over the community, Bisbee was not destined to become a "company town." It expanded in every direction with little regard for overall planning. Homes were built in tiers on hillsides so steep that one man's yard was even with his neighbor's roof. It was said that any chewer with talent could sit on his porch and

(Top) *The Inn at Castle Rock was built by Bisbee's first mayor. Interestingly, it was constructed over an open mine shaft that filled with water from a natural spring.*
JERRY JACKA

(Above) *Bisbee was primarily a mining town, but nearby ranchers on both sides of the Mexican border made it their community, too. These Mexican cowboys got into a photo-worthy formation on a downtown street in the early 1880s.*
ARIZONA HISTORICAL SOCIETY

spit tobacco juice into his neighbor's chimney.

While the company was erecting edifices of propriety in the town's main canyon, a less respectable element was constructing saloons and brothels in an adjoining area that became famous as Brewery Gulch.

In 1889, a railroad was constructed from Bisbee around the southwestern end of the Mule Mountains to an existing line at Fairbank (see p. 124), further reducing the cost of getting smelted copper to market.

In 1901, the only serious rival to the Copper Queen arrived when the Calumet and Arizona Company opened several mines in the Warren District, including the highly successful Irish Mag (supposedly named by a grateful patron of a prostitute with that moniker). Two towns, Lowell and Jiggerville, grew near the new mines.

Also in 1901, Copper Queen Consolidated extended a company-owned railroad, the El Paso and Southwestern, 25 miles to Douglas, where a smelter was built. A year

later, the Calumet and Arizona also erected a smelter there, thus ending the choking pollution that had engulfed Bisbee. As it became a far more pleasant place to live and work, Bisbee became known by the sobriquet "Little San Francisco."

Like the City by the Bay, Bisbee had its disasters. A year after the 1906 San Francisco Earthquake, a fire roared across Chihuahua Hill, destroying residences and many businesses along Brewery Gulch. A year later, another conflagration wiped out buildings of Bisbee's upper Main Street and dozens of homes. Many structures had to be dynamited to create a firebreak. The estimated loss was $500,000.

Because the denuded hills above the town could not absorb rainfall as they once had, Bisbee also suffered repeatedly from flooding. In addition to natural disasters, a series of typhoid epidemics swept through town.

Nevertheless, Bisbee prospered. In addition to copper,

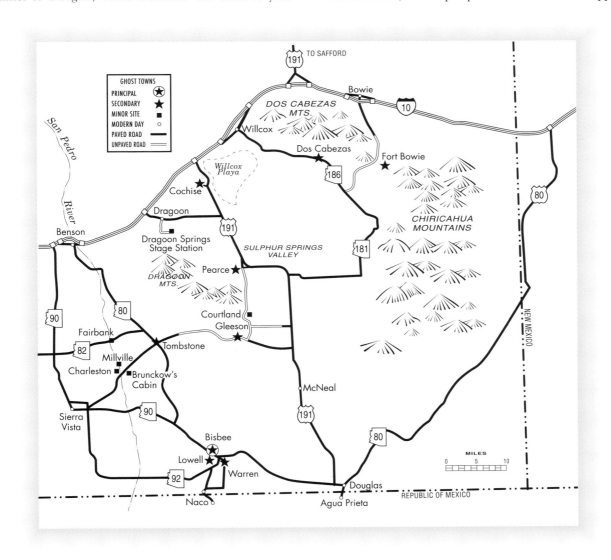

the town became the shipping center for surrounding cattle ranches and the financial center for American-owned mines at Cananea and Nacozari in Sonora, Mexico.

In 1907, Calumet and Arizona Mining and Copper Queen Consolidated joined forces to create the Warren Company. Its task was to build Warren, a company town for the expanding mining populace. The central feature of Warren was the Vista, a six-block-long greenbelt with exclusive homes lining the park and lesser ones extending in either direction. At the apex of the Vista, with a commanding view of the area, stood the elegant Douglas mansion.

Warren had the city planning that Bisbee lacked, with water from the mine irrigating dozens of trees planted

near its residences, company offices, stores, schools, and baseball park.

The Warren-Bisbee Railway began operating in 1908. Known simply as "the streetcar," it connected Warren, Lowell, and Bisbee for a 10-cent fare and took about a half-hour. With it, the three towns were linked in a tangible, cosmopolitan way.

Bisbee's fortunes took an important turn in 1917. Phelps Dodge, now operating under its own name, bought the Calumet and Arizona shares in the Warren Company and emerged as the dominant power in Bisbee. In addition, Phelps Dodge opened the Sacramento Pit, its first attempt at open-pit mining. That process was to add almost 60 years to Bisbee's mining life.

The third event of 1917 was not as positive. With World War I raging, Bisbee miners went on strike, led by the Industrial Workers of the World (also called the "Wobblies"). The I.W.W. was accused of subversive, even Communist, leanings and deemed by some as un-American. Bisbee law officers, aided by 1,500 sympathizers, rounded up 1,200 strikers and "outside agitators," herding them into cattle cars. The train unceremoniously deposited them in the New Mexico desert to fend for themselves. A subsequent commission from Washington D.C. deplored the so-called Bisbee Deportation but could not find any specific law that had been broken.

Between World War I and the Great Depression the Sacramento Pit kept Bisbee going, but the pit closed in

1931. That year Phelps Dodge acquired the failing Calumet and Arizona Mining Company, thereby becoming the undisputed leader in the Warren District. Underground mining kept Bisbee hanging on through the Depression until World War II rekindled the demand for copper. Bisbee's fortunes improved as prices rose.

In 1951, Phelps Dodge opened the remarkable Lavender Pit, named not for the lavender-colored hues of its walls but for Mine Manager Harrison Lavender. A mammoth undertaking for its day, the new pit extended southeast from the Sacramento Pit and required the realignment of U.S. Route 80 (now State Route 80). It also obliterated small communities and made Lowell into a business district whose main street led to a chasm.

The Lavender Pit also had an adverse effect on Warren. When the company town was created, it was far removed from the mines. But the incredible volume of dump space needed for the pit brought the mine to Warren's doorstep. The Douglas home lost its imposing presence at the top of the Vista. Instead, the mansion was dwarfed by Leaching Dump No. 7, which still looms behind the imposing residence like a grotesque sandpile for the world's most spoiled kid.

Eventually the Lavender Pit also played out, closing with the night shift of December 14, 1974. The Copper Queen Mine, the underground wonder that George Warren lost on a bet almost a century before, ceased operations six months later. Bisbee had produced more

(**Above**) *While modern Bisbee has just 6,000 citizens, it is increasingly popular with retirees and remains the Cochise County seat.*
JERRY JACKA
(**Far Left**) *Downtown Bisbee retains much of the flavor of yesteryear. The mines have closed, but the city has become a mecca for visitors.*
PHILIP VARNEY
(**Below**) *In its heyday, Bisbee was a city of 35,000 and the mining, commercial, financial, and cultural center of southeastern Arizona.*
ARIZONA HISTORICAL SOCIETY

than 8 billion pounds of copper worth about $2 billion. In the process, the mines had also yielded 3.9 million pounds of lead, 3.8 million pounds of zinc, 2.7 million ounces of gold, and more than 1 million ounces of silver. By 1975 Bisbee was just another place that had joined the long list of former mining camps on their way to obscurity.

Or so it might have seemed. Bisbee, which could easily

have become a derelict, has rebounded, not retired. After the closing of the mines, Phelps Dodge relocated many of its workers to other operations. The town retained the county seat, and some lifelong residents chose to stay. They were joined by retirees who found comparatively inexpensive housing in a lovely location, and by young artists, photographers, and craftsmakers who began small businesses. The result is a sometimes uneasy blend of the old and the new, the conservative and the progressive. The overall effect is positive, however, since everyone shares the goal of keeping Bisbee alive. The population, which initially dropped from 35,000 to 5,500, has increased to about 6,000 as of this writing. Real estate prices have climbed significantly in the last decade. Bisbee is back.

Start a visit to Bisbee at the scenic turnout on State Route 80 overlooking the town. The original Dunn claim is on the hill behind the turnout. Glorious Bisbee spreads out below.

The first stop is the Bisbee Mining and Historical Museum, located in the 1897 headquarters of the Copper Queen Consolidated Mining Company. The museum gives an excellent historical overview of the Warren District with displays, memorabilia, and even a simulated mine tunnel.

Available at the museum are three informative brochures describing enjoyable walking tours of Main Street, Brewery Gulch, and School Hill. Each gives clear directions, pointing out historic buildings and providing insiders' anecdotes about Bisbee. Those who prefer to wander should be certain to see the library-post office, Copper Queen Hotel, Pythian Castle, Muheim Block, and Muheim Heritage House (a restored museum piece). Numerous other residences, churches, and commercial buildings showcase period architecture.

The underground Queen Mine tour, which starts across the highway from downtown Bisbee, is one of the most informative mine tours in the West. Visitors wear yellow slickers and miners' hard hats (complete with lamps) as they straddle the seats of a narrow-gauge personnel carrier into the mine that registers a

(**Above**) *Miners and carpenters joined forces in the excavation of the Copper Queen Mine at Bisbee, one of the West's richest producers.*
ARIZONA HISTORICAL SOCIETY
(**Right, Above**) *Toilet cars enabled miners to comply with the strict rules of underground sanitation.*
SHARLOT HALL MUSEUM
(**Right**) *This carbide lamp was used to light the Copper Queen's dark cavern.*
JOHN DREW

constant temperature of 47 degrees. The guides know what they're talking about. As former miners, they give the experience an air of authenticity few others could. Phelps Dodge leases the mine to Bisbee for $1 a year, but visitors get the real bargain.

The most ghostly remains are at Lowell at the southeastern lip of the Lavender Pit. The Lowell Theater, an old service station, and other buildings dating from about 1904 sit by themselves, bypassed by the realigned highway and isolated by the pit. Southeast of Lowell is the Hub, a large traffic circle with "spokes" heading off to various locations. Just before the spoke that returns to Bisbee a side road leads to Evergreen Cemetery, a fascinating testament to the diversity of those who came in search of opportunity: Italians, Hispanics, Serbs, Welsh, Irish, and Cornish, among others. Many of the graves were moved to Lowell from the old Bisbee Cemetery, which was located in Brewery Gulch at the present site of the City Park before being closed in 1915.

Warren has many homes of widely varied architectural styles along the Vista and near the Douglas mansion. Several of the better-preserved homes are now bed-and-breakfast establishments. At the south end of town is the antiquated ball park, looking as if Ty Cobb, Babe Ruth, and countless others might occasionally sneak into this "field of dreams."

Bisbee, however, remains the prime attraction. Its oddities are its charm. A garage is built over a drainage ditch. A stairway seems to lead nowhere, until unexpectedly a large residential area comes into view. Everyone has a post office box — a mailman would never survive home delivery. The customized fire truck has an extra-short turning radius to make the required hairpin turns. The old four-story high school is on a hill so steep that each floor has a ground-level door. Perhaps Bisbee was "Queen of the Copper Camps," but it will always have the appeal of "Little San Francisco."

WHEN YOU GO: Bisbee is 94 miles southeast of Tucson via Interstate 10 and State Route 80.

Tombstone Area Ghosts

Tombstone, along with the Grand Canyon, is known to tourists from around the world. More than 200,000 visitors come here annually, taking videos of the staged gunfights, and returning home having seen the "real Old West." Tombstone does have lots of hype, but it also has lots of history and considerable charm for the ghost town visitor.

In 1877, prospector Ed Schieffelin stood at Camp Huachuca and gazed longingly at the hills to the northeast. Their rich color looked promising to him, and he expressed a desire to do a little digging. A soldier, well aware of the Apache warriors who controlled the area, told him, "All you'll find in those hills is your tombstone." In February of 1878, Schieffelin set out alone to seek his fortune. He eventually found a rich ledge of silver ore, and, remembering the soldier's remark, filed two claims: the Tombstone and the Graveyard.

In order to show the ore to his brother, Al, and have it assayed, Schieffelin traveled all the way to Signal (now a ghost townsite about 170 air miles from Tombstone). The brothers returned with Signal assayer Richard K. Gird, who had recognized the value of the ore and persuaded the brothers to let him become a partner. Upon returning, Ed went out and found two more silver streaks in two days and filed claims for the Lucky Cuss (which was what he considered himself), and the Toughnut (which he figured would be a difficult ledge to follow, or "a tough nut to crack"). An estimated $40 million in silver (worth about $1.7 billion in today's dollars) was extracted from these and other area mines between 1880 and 1886.

Entrepreneur John B. "Pie" Allen was a leader in

Legendary Allen Street in Tombstone was a center of activity in the 1880s when "The Town Too Tough to Die" was at its boisterous best. In the foreground is the famed Crystal Palace saloon, which featured Marshall Virgil Earp's office upstairs.
PHILIP VARNEY

turning a disjointed series of camps with names like Watervale, Richmond, Tank Hill, and Gird Camp into Tombstone, one of the West's largest and most genteel towns. Yes, despite its fame as the site of the Gunfight at the OK Corral, Tombstone actually was a rather cultured place. It had four churches, a school, two banks, a newspaper (the *Epitaph*), an opera, and a population of 15,000. The violence of the OK Corral, which lasted but a few seconds and resulted in three deaths, was a rarity. Raucous behavior was much more common in Charleston and Millville.

Charleston and Millville existed because Tombstone had plenty of silver but not enough water. Since water is vital to the milling process, Richard Gird selected a mill site along the east bank of the San Pedro River, nine miles southwest of Tombstone. The place became known as Millville. Charleston, a town that supported the

(**Top**) *Folks at Fairbank, a Tombstone satellite settled in 1882, did their trading at the Fairbank Commercial Company. The building has been stabilized.*
PHILIP VARNEY
(**Above**) *Mining in the 1880s required a lot of animals. This mule train is carrying ore from a Tombstone mine.*
ARIZONA HISTORICAL SOCIETY

milling operations, grew up on the west bank of the river.

Charleston eventually had a population of about 400. Soldiers from Camp (later Fort) Huachuca often came to Charleston to drink alongside miners, and occasionally rustlers and ruffians. Charleston was definitely not for the faint of heart.

Fairbank was another satellite community to Tombstone. It came into existence in 1882 with construction of the New Mexico and Arizona Railroad. This short line was a link between the Southern Pacific tracks in Benson and the border town of Nogales. Fairbank was created where the track turned west. Its proximity also turned Fairbank into Tombstone's supply depot. Named for Nathaniel Kellogg Fairbank, a Chicago grain broker and a founding member of the Grand Central Mining Company in Tombstone, the town probably never had more than 100 people. It did, however, have a maze of tracks. Three separate railroads eventually located depots there. Besides the line to Nogales, one went to Bisbee, and a branch eventually extended into Tombstone. Because of the railroads, Fairbank outlived both Charleston and Millville.

During futile attempts to reopen Tombstone's mines, Fairbank was the site of a train robbery involving one of Arizona's most respected lawmen, Jeff Milton. In February of 1900, Milton rode in an express car guarding a Wells Fargo box. A gang with Billy Stiles and Burt Alvord, both lawmen gone bad, rushed the train at its stop in Fairbank. Milton fatally wounded one of the five robbers. Then a shot splintered his left arm, but he managed to throw the strongbox key out into the brush. A crowd gathered, and the robbery was aborted. One bandit escaped to Mexico, but the other three were captured. Milton was taken by rail to a surgeon in San Francisco. Told that his arm had to be amputated, he said, "The man who cuts off my arm will be a dead man." Not surprisingly, his arm was spared and he regained partial use of it.

Now, with several good 1880s buildings remaining, Fairbank is part of the San Pedro Riparian National Conservation Area under the Bureau of Land Management (BLM). The Fairbank Commercial Company, a large adobe structure, was in danger of collapse, but BLM stabilized it. A few houses and a gypsum-block school, circa 1920, stand north of the mercantile. The public can take self-guided tours, and an on-site host opens the gate at sunrise and closes at sunset. (520) 439-6400.

Tombstone, meanwhile, proved to be very enduring. Fires ravaged the main street in 1881 and 1882, but each time the town merely rebuilt more elaborate edifices. Ed

Tombstone had its epitaph), Nellie Cashman's Boarding House, Fire House Engine Company No.1, and the railroad depot, now the town's library.

On the northwest end of Tombstone is the famous Boothill Cemetery. West of town, past the current Tombstone Cemetery, is a pyramid-like stone cairn that marks the grave of Ed Schieffelin, who requested that his remains be returned to the site where he spent two nights hiding from Apaches before making his famous strike.

Brunckow's cabin, called "the bloodiest cabin in Arizona history," is a historic spot located along the route from Tombstone to Sierra Vista shortly before Charleston. (The sparse ruins are situated on a knoll 8 miles southwest of Tombstone, about 40 yards down S. Brunckow Road). More than 20 years before Ed Schieffelin headed into the Tombstone hills, Brunckow was already there. A German exile, Brunckow worked a

Schieffelin, who preferred the role of prospector to that of wealthy mine owner, left Tombstone for new adventures in the Yukon.

Then in 1886, the water that had been so scarce turned, quite literally, into a flood. Shafts penetrated the underground water table, inundating operations and closing the mines. Charleston and Millville were dead, and "The Town Too Tough to Die" suffered a grievous, but not fatal, wound.

Although Tombstone's population declined drastically, the town hung on. Attempts to reopen the mines began in the 1890s and lasted past the turn of the century, when flooding again ended operations. When the town lost the county seat in 1929 to Bisbee, the *Graham County Guardian* proclaimed the event "the death knell of Tombstone." The pockets of silver in the hills, however, have been replaced by silver in the pockets of tourists, and Tombstone is alive and well.

The 1882 Territorial Courthouse, now a state park, features numerous historical displays, including a restored courtroom and gallows. Another worthwhile building is St. Paul's Episcopal Church, the oldest Protestant church in Arizona, which dates from 1882.

Several structures of historical significance stand along Allen Street (named for John Allen), including the famous Bird Cage Theater, built in 1881 as a combination theater-dancehall-saloon; the Crystal Palace, an 1879 saloon that housed the upstairs offices of Town Marshal Virgil Earp and Sheriff Johnny Behan; and the OK Corral, which was immortalized in one turbulent moment of gunfire.

Other historic buildings include the office of the *Tombstone Epitaph* (founder John P. Clum claimed every

(Left, Above) *Stars of the New York stage made appearances at Tombstone's Bird Cage Theater in the late 19th century.*
(Above) *Charleston's ghostly ruins hide in a mesquite-filled bosque near the San Pedro River.*
BOTH BY PHILIP VARNEY

125

small mine near his cabin. He managed to escape the wrath of the Apache, but not that of bandits from across the border. He was murdered at his cabin, the first of 21 people known to have been killed there. When Ed Schieffelin came through from Camp Huachuca, he spent one night in the abandoned adobe house. Later the cabin became a favorite meeting place for desperadoes, who enjoyed the panoramic views that gave them early warning of annoyances — like posses.

WHEN YOU GO: Tombstone is 69 miles southeast of Tucson via Interstate 10 and State Route 80. Charleston and Millville are 9.4 miles southwest of Tombstone on the Charleston Road. Their scant remains are part of the San Pedro River Resource Conservation Area. Millville can be reached by walking north along a trail that leaves from a fence east of the railroad tracks paralleling the San Pedro River. The stone embankments for two mills are visible from the highway. To find the crumbling adobe walls of Charleston, walk west from Millville, cross the tracks, and find a safe place to climb down from the railroad bed to the San Pedro, which you will need to cross. The ruins are best found using a GPS waypoint (see p. 135). Both Charleston and Millville have fragile ruins that are protected by federal law. Please leave the sites undisturbed. Fairbank is 10 miles northwest of Tombstone on State Route 82.

(Above) *Now a National Historic Site, Fort Bowie once guarded a precious water supply and protected travelers crossing southeastern Arizona Territory.*
PHILIP VARNEY
(Right, Above) *A cavalry troop rides out of Fort Bowie to protect the vital stagecoach road across southern Arizona Territory. Established in 1862, Fort Bowie was abandoned in 1894.*
NATIONAL ARCHIVES
(Right) *Apache leaders Geronimo, right, and Natches, are shown at Fort Bowie after their surrender.*
ARIZONA HISTORICAL SOCIETY

The Ghost Town Trail

A popular drive out of Tombstone is known to people in Cochise County as The Ghost Town Trail. This extended version of that trip adds three extra sites, giving visitors a greater variety of attractions: a ghost fort, four mining camps, three stage stations, and a railroad town.

Fort Bowie was established to protect the most vital of desert resources: water. Water was a scarce commodity for immigrants and U.S. mail carriers crossing the southern part of Arizona, and Apache Spring was a reliable source. Its name, however, reveals the travelers' problem. The once-friendly Chiricahua tribe was in no mood to share the spring after the U.S. Army betrayed Cochise and killed six of his relatives. Within 24 hours of that

betrayal, Apaches attacked a Butterfield stage and a wagon train, killing 14 settlers. After repeated skirmishes, in 1862 the Army established Camp Bowie adjacent to Apache Spring.

A truce with the Chiricahua Apache in 1872 brought a temporary end to the conflicts. But Cochise's death in 1874 and the removal of the tribe to the San Carlos Reservation in 1876 — despite promises they would not have to leave their traditional territory — broke the peace. Geronimo and other renegade warriors bolted the reservation and began a 10-year campaign of raids from Mexican hideaways in the Sierra Madres.

Camp Bowie, upgraded to fort status in 1879, became a modern outpost with such necessities as a bakery, hospital, and telegraph office. It also boasted luxuries like a tailor shop, a billiard parlor-beer hall, and a tennis court.

But the most impressive extravagance was the seven-bedroom, two-story Victorian edifice that served as the Commanding Officer's Quarters. Its first occupant, Maj. Eugene Beaumont, complained, "The large amount of useless and unnecessary ornamentation has been of great expense and waste of time . . . ."

Geronimo's surrender in 1886 made the fort expendable. It was abandoned in 1894. The property was thoroughly scavenged for items of value, and only adobe walls remain today. Now a National Historic Site, Fort Bowie is preserved in a state of arrested decay, meaning there are no plans to restore the site to its earlier grandeur.

Visitors to the fort must take a one-and-a-half mile hike from a parking area (for information on handicapped access, call 520-847-2500). The hike is a delightful way to get into the 1880s feeling as one passes the

(Above) *Dos Cabezas, pictured here in 1924, was an important stagecoach stop more than a century ago.*
Jeremy Rowe Collection
(Left) *The remains of this adobe house at Dos Cabezas, now a sleepy roadside community along State Route 186, must have witnessed some exciting days of early Arizona history. In the distance behind the residence stands the only "head" of Dos Cabezas visible from the townsite.*
Philip Varney

127

ruins of a Butterfield stage depot, the probable foundations of the Indian Agency built for Tom Jeffords (the white man most trusted by Cochise and reputedly his "blood brother"), the post cemetery, and Apache Spring itself. The ruins of the fort are ghostly and beautiful, without power lines and parking lots to destroy the mood.

Dos Cabezas, where Ewell Spring is located, was the next dependable source of water west of Apache Spring. Another stage depot was built here, and in the late 1870s gold and silver were found in the Dos Cabezas Mountains (Spanish for "Two Heads," for the prominent twin peaks) above the spring. The resulting town took its name from the peaks.

On the highway through Dos Cabezas one can see an adobe commercial building still under roof, several plastered adobe walls, remnants of residences, and some occupied buildings of recent vintage. A picturesque cemetery is on a hillside west of town.

Cochise is an example of a ghost town that was not a mining camp. It was created in the early 1880s as a water and fuel stop along the Southern Pacific Railroad. In 1882 railroad telegrapher John Rath built the Cochise Hotel to serve the railroad crews and also put a Wells Fargo office in the front room. As ranching increased in the Sulphur Springs Valley and mining activity began in nearby Pearce and Johnson, Cochise became an established town with a peak population of about 3,000. A post office was granted in 1896 and still operates.

Cochise had one day in the headlines. On September 9, 1889, Billy Stiles and Matt Burts of the Stiles-Alvord gang robbed a train here. An informer's tip led to their capture, but five months later, the gang was back at work in Fairbank (see p. 124).

In May of 1903, Cochise once again became a hub of activity when the Arizona and Colorado Railroad built a branch line from Cochise to Pearce, eventually extending the tracks to Gleeson.

Besides the post office, Cochise today has about 25 residents, a school, a boarded-up church, and two of the better adobe buildings in rural Arizona: the Cochise Country Store and the Cochise Hotel (listed on the National Historic Register). The store is occupied but closed to the public; the hotel is open for meals and lodging (both by reservation only). Its guest rooms are furnished in the period, and the old harness shop nearby is a fully furnished vacation rental. After dinner, there's only the sunset and silence – a silence broken occasionally by the roar of a passing freight powered by a diesel locomotive that never stops for water or coal.

Dragoon Springs was another Butterfield stage station, the site of one of the most amazing will-to-live stories in Arizona history.

Station manager Silas St. John was entrusted to build a depot at Dragoon Springs near the northwest tip of the Dragoon Mountains (named for the Third U.S. Cavalry Dragoons that patrolled the mountains between Fort Bowie and Fort Huachuca). In September of 1858, three Mexican laborers turned on their American crew members, killing three and severing St. John's left arm with an ax. He also suffered an ax wound to the hip. Nonetheless, he fought off his attackers and defended his dead or dying companions from buzzards and coyotes for three

(**Above**) *Built in 1894, this old store is one of several surviving buildings in Pearce that lure ghost town buffs to the area.*
PHILIP VARNEY
(**Facing Page**) *This opening through an adobe wall at Pearce serves as a window to the Old West.*
JERRY JACKA

129

days. Finally help arrived and a surgeon was summoned. Dr. B.J. Irwin rode from Fort Buchanan, almost 120 miles away. He operated on St. John, saving his life.

The stage station may be reached via N. Old Ranch Road, which heads west and then south 2.3 miles from Dragoon to Jordan Canyon. Turn east and go 1.1 miles to a cattle-proof fenced-off area. The rock ruins, and a small cemetery in which are buried Confederate soldiers who died in a 1862 skirmish with Apaches, are a short distance beyond the gate. A high-clearance vehicle is necessary for the final 1.1 miles.

Pearce was named for Jimmie Pearce, a man who tired of being a Tombstone miner after the boom years waned and pickings were slim. He and his wife, who ran a boardinghouse, were saving their money to buy a piece of the great outdoors. They managed, finally, to purchase some ranch land northeast of Tombstone. One day in 1894, while out surveying his spread, Jimmie found free gold on the side of a hill. He was back in the mining business, but as an owner, not a laborer.

A town grew at the base of Jimmie Pearce's Commonwealth Mine. A post office opened in 1896 and the population swelled to about 1,500 as commercial businesses, which eventually included a motion-picture theater, lined both sides of a long main street.

Jimmie Pearce sold the Commonwealth for $250,000. His wife, remembering harder times, inserted a clause into the contract granting her the sole right to operate a boardinghouse at the mine, which remained open into the 1930s.

Several buildings remain from Pearce's heyday, including the post office, a school, a jail, a few ruins and foundations, and the remarkable Old Store, built in 1894 by the Soto Brothers and Renaud. The mercantile is a large adobe building with a high false front and an elaborate tin facade.

The Pearce Cemetery is west of town along Middlemarch Road, a trail across the Dragoon Mountains taken by soldiers trekking between Fort Bowie and Fort Huachuca in the 1870s and '80s.

Courtland is the only community on the Ghost Town Trail that is completely deserted. It also has the sparsest remnants, with only a concrete jail, a collapsing store, stone walls, foundations, and considerable mining evidence.

Once, however, Courtland thrived. In 1909 several hundred people swarmed to the region as the Calumet and Arizona, Copper Queen, Leadville, and Great Western mining companies all began operations. The Great Western was owned by W.J. Young, who named the town for his brother Courtland. Eventually home to about 2,000 people, the settlement had a post office,

newspaper (the *Courtland Arizonan*), movie theater, butcher shop, ice cream parlor, pool hall, Wells Fargo office, the Southern Arizona Auto Company (a local Stevens-Duryea agency), and the Mexico and Colorado Railroad, a branch line extending north from Douglas.

The town survived into the Depression but lost its post office in 1942. By that time many of the buildings had already been moved or razed.

Warning: Many open shafts, some unfenced, are near the townsite. Those walking around Courtland should exercise extreme caution.

Gleeson and the hills at the southern end of the Dragoon Mountains had long been mined by the Indians for the decorative turquoise. When white men came in the 1870s, they found copper, lead, and silver as well, but they still named their camp Turquoise. The town received a post office in 1890, but the mines closed down and the town was abandoned after Jimmie Pearce found gold at the Commonwealth claim in 1894. Then in 1900, a Pearce miner and Irishman named John Gleeson prospected the Turquoise area and filed claims for the Copper Belle mine. Other mines with names like Silver Belle, Brother Jonathan, Pejon, and Defiance joined the Copper Belle. The townsite was moved from the hills down onto the flats to be closer to a more reliable water supply, and Turquoise, which had lost its post office in 1894, reopened as Gleeson.

John Gleeson sold out by 1914, but the boom continued and copper production rose due to World War I. After the war, prices fell, production declined, and the mines shut down. The post office closed its doors for the

last time in 1939.

Gleeson is well worth exploring. Just north of its main road are the long adobe ruins of the hospital, with mining evidence in the hills behind. Down the street from the hospital stands a saloon-store that had an off-again, on-again existence for decades and is closed at this writing. Across the street south of the store are the ruins of the jail (virtually identical to the one at Courtland) and the foundations of the school.

A road heading north from the store passes the adobe ruins of the Musso house (posted against trespassing). A prohibition-era rumor suggested the Mussos sold bootleg liquor and stored it beneath a shallow fishpond in the backyard. It may have been more than rumor — when I first visited the house in the 1970s, I found the fishpond with a kind of vault visible underneath it.

The Gleeson Cemetery, the final stop along the Ghost Town Trail, is west of town on the main road to Tombstone.

WHEN YOU GO: The trailhead to Fort Bowie is 113 miles southeast of Tucson via I-10. Take the Bowie Exit and follow signs to the site. Dos Cabezas is 16 miles from Fort Bowie. Cochise is 14 miles southwest of Willcox on U.S. Route 191 (formerly U.S. 666). Pearce is 16 miles south of Cochise. The dirt road heading south from Pearce leads to Courtland and Gleeson. Tombstone is 15 miles west of Gleeson. The entire Ghost Town Trail from the Fort Bowie trailhead to Tombstone (without the side trip to the Dragoon Springs Stage Station) covers about 90 miles. All but 35 miles are paved. Under normal conditions the graded dirt roads are suitable for a passenger car.

Index

The Tom Reed Mine had periodic "clean-ups," in which the mill operation was stopped and workers pried every bit of gold from nooks and crannies of the machinery. This 1913 clean-up produced five cone-shaped molds of gold valued at $110,000.
MOHAVE COUNTY HISTORICAL SOCIETY

GPS Waypoints, Topographic Maps, and Specific Directions

The greatest improvement in ghost town exploring since the initial publication of this book in 1994 is the advent of GPS (Global Positioning System) technology. As roads change or as formerly uninhabited areas become settled, the position of a ghost town remains, unless something dramatic like an open pit erases a site (which has, in fact, occurred many times in Arizona). The following waypoints, more than a hundred of them, were hand entered: I did not use software maps in my computer to generate them. They were all created as I stood in front of, inside, or at least near (when a site was on private property) the ghost town in question.

The benefit to the back roads enthusiast is incalculable. If you have a GPS receiver and know how to use it, you can enter these waypoints and drive or walk right to them.

Some are not as crucial as others, to be sure, but several waypoints mean the difference between finding and missing a site.

Remember, as GPS users know, there are "good" satellite days and "bad" ones. But even on a "bad" day, you should be within a matter of a few dozen feet, if not closer, of the place you have been seeking.

United States Geological Survey (USGS) topographic maps (topos) can be helpful aids as well. They are generally available at outdoor and sporting goods stores.

If you're not GPS oriented, four destinations in this book require specific directions, as small mistakes can take you off the intended route. Accordingly, I have included expanded directions to the Swansea, Las Guijas, Sunnyside, and Helvetia sites.

Chapter One

Jerome [Cottonwood, Clarkdale topos]
N 34° 45.068' W 112° 06.972' in front of Conner Hotel
N 34° 45.183' W 112° 06.287' cemetery
N 34° 45.248' W 112° 06.735' Douglas mansion gate

Clarkdale [Clarkdale topographic map]
N 34° 46.274' W 112° 03.483' downtown on Main Street
N 34° 46.498' W 112° 02.691' Clark mansion
N 34° 46.750' W 112° 03.251' Patio Town

Clemenceau [Cottonwood topographic map]
N 34° 44.389' W 112° 01.616' in front of museum

Humboldt [Humboldt, Mayer topos]
N 34° 30.107' W 112° 14.394' downtown, Main and Prescott streets

Mayer [Mayer topographic map]
N 34° 24.005' W 112° 14.315' old downtown at Main and Oak streets

Cordes [Cleator topographic map]
N 34° 18.205' W 112° 09.982' in front of former store

Bumble Bee [Bumble Bee topographic map]
N 34° 12.068' W 112° 09.175' in front of former school

Cleator [Cleator topographic map]
N 34° 16.688' W 112° 14.039' in front of store

Crown King [Crown King topographic map]
N 34° 12.339' W 112° 20.313' in front of store/post office
N 34° 12.770' W 112° 20.559' inside cemetery

Bradshaw City [Crown King topographic map]
N 34° 11.809' W 112° 21.334' townsite sign
N 34° 11.555' W 112° 21.232' turnoff to cemetery
N 34° 11.512' W 112° 21.376' cemetery

Walker [Groom Creek, Poland Jct. topos]
N 34° 27.540' W 112° 22.541' townsite sign
N 34° 27.450' W 112° 22.390' charcoal kiln

Maxton [Groom Creek topographic map]
N 34° 25.625' W 112° 25.734' store ruin

Senator [Groom Creek topographic map]
N 34° 25.619' W 112° 26.034' turnoff to mill ruins

Palace Station [Groom Creek topographic map]
N 34° 22.601' W 112° 24.596' old cabin's historical sign

Chapter Two

Vulture [Vulture Mine topographic map]
N 33° 48.987' W 112° 49.716' entrance gate to mining site

Stanton [Yarnell topographic map]
N 34° 09.733' W 112° 43.873' entrance to town

Weaver [Yarnell topographic map]
N 34° 09.296' W 112° 42.423' in front of former post office

Octave [Yarnell topographic map]
N 34° 08.575' W 112° 42.666' gate in front of townsite

Congress [Congress topographic map]
N 34° 09.573' W 112° 50.672' on highway at Congress Jct.
N 34° 11.892' W 112° 51.352' entrance to Congress Mine

N 34° 11.630' W 112° 51.011' pioneer cemetery

Gold Leaf [Date Ck. Ranch SE, SW topos]
Mine N 34° 01.282' W 113° 07.605' Mining World entrance

Humbug [Columbia topographic map]
N 34° 03.213' W 112° 19.372' in townsite (private)

Chapter Three

Oatman [Oatman topographic map]
N 35° 01.579' W 114° 23.015' on highway, near Oatman Hotel

Goldroad [Oatman, Mount Nutt topos]
N 35° 02.439' W 114° 22.392' easternmost ruins
N 35° 02.734' W 114° 22.830' westernmost ruins

Chloride [Chloride topographic map]
N 35° 24.862' W 114° 11.971' Tennessee Ave. and 2nd St.

Mineral Park [Cerbat, Chloride topos]
N 35° 22.182' W 114° 09.782' post office ruins on right
N 35° 22.366' W 114° 09.372' town remnants

Cerbat [Cerbat topographic map]
N 35° 18.208' W 114° 08.098' within townsite

Chapter Four

Swansea [Swansea topographic map]
N 34° 04.237' W 113° 53.220' site of Midway
N 34° 08.260' W 113° 55.639' turnoff NW of Midway
N 34° 10.165' W 113° 50.659' company store ruin

Specific Directions: From Bouse, take Main Street northeast across the railroad tracks. When it curves, it becomes Rayder Road. The pavement turns to graded dirt as it becomes the Swansea Road, eventually crossing the Central Arizona Project Canal. The now-vanished site of Midway, a former water stop on the short line railroad that connected Bouse and Swansea, is almost 13 miles from Bouse. It is marked with a large BLM sign. Take the left fork and go to an intersection 18 miles from Bouse. Take the right fork northeast for 7 more miles to Swansea. (You'll pass over an aboveground pipeline 1.5 miles beyond this intersection.) High-clearance vehicle required. This is a fair-weather trip only.

Yuma [Yuma East topographic map]
Crossing N 32° 43.631' W 114° 37.409' state park entrance

Fort Yuma [Yuma East topographic map]
N 32° 43.953' W 114° 37.052' Quechan Indian Museum

Yuma Territorial [Yuma East topographic map]
Prison N 32° 43.637' W 114° 36.869' prison entrance

Picacho [Picacho Ariz./Calif. topo map]
N 33° 01.252' W 114° 37.067' cemetery
N 33° 01.314' W 114° 36.671' parking area for historic tour

Ehrenberg [Blythe Calif./Ariz. topo map]
N 33° 36.334' W 114° 31.421' historic cemetery

Quartzsite [Quartzsite topographic map]
N 33° 39.864' W 114° 14.178' historic cemetery

Chapter Five

Clifton [Clifton topographic map]
N 33° 03.363' W 109° 18.260' in front of historical society
N 33° 04.959' W 109° 18.233' at Potter Ranch

134

Klondyke	[Klondyke topographic map]	
	N 33° 50.179' W 110° 19.951'	in front of store
Copper Hill	[Globe topographic map]	
	N 32° 25.660' W 110° 46.054'	in middle of townsite
Cochran	[North Butte topographic map]	
	N 33° 06.340' W 111° 09.266'	viewpoint for kilns to the west
	N 33° 06.573' W 111° 09.025'	townsite at railroad tracks

Chapter Six

Silverbell	[Silverbell West topographic map]	
	N 32° 24.211' W 111° 32.732'	driving across slag
	N 32° 25.705' W 111° 33.460'	viewpoint; look east to mining evidence
	N 32° 26.160' W 111° 33.579'	turnoff to cemetery; go west
	N 32° 26.154' W 111° 33.681'	cemetery
Sasco	[Samaniego Hills topographic map]	
	N 32° 32.124' W 111° 26.418'	at foot of smelter stack
	N 32° 32.184' W 111° 25.904'	Rockland Hotel ruin
	N 32° 32.678' W 111° 25.927'	cemetery
Copper Creek	[Oak Grove Canyon and Rhodes Peak topographic maps]	
	N 32° 45.197' W 110° 28.677'	store steps and foundation
	N 32° 45.183' W 110° 28.380'	leave car in this area
	N 32° 45.197' W 110° 28.246'	take left fork to walk along creek
	N 32° 45.466' W 110° 27.273'	Sibley mansion
	N 32° 45.515' W 110° 27.198'	store across creek from mansion

Chapter Seven

Cerro Colorado	[Cerro Colorado topographic map]	
	N 31° 39.566' W 111° 16.143'	turnoff to Poston's grave
	N 31° 39.645' W 111° 16.368'	Poston's grave
Las Guijas	[Cerro Colorado and Las Guijas topographic maps]	
	N 31° 39.427' W 111° 19.340'	water trailer on way to site
	N 31° 39.181' W 111° 20.502'	corral and line house
	N 31° 40.091' W 111° 22.851'	first foundation at site
	N 31° 40.166' W 111° 22.824'	paddy wagon

Specific Directions: From Poston's grave at Cerro Colorado, drive west, taking the left fork in .2 of a mile onto a much lesser road. Do not take the right to Rancho Seco. After 2.2 more miles, take the left fork that parallels the wash. You'll know you're on the correct road when you pass a tanker truck trailer. Beyond the trailer 1.1 miles, cross a wash and take the right fork that goes around corrals, a windmill, and a vacant house. Continue on the main road for 2.3 more miles, where there is a road going right marked with stacked boulders. Do not go right; continue straight ahead for .6 of a mile to the first foundation of Las Guijas. A high-clearance vehicle is required.

Arivaca	[Arivaca topographic map]	
	N 31° 34.498' W 111° 19.815'	in front of mercantile
Oro Blanco	[Bartlett Mtn. topographic map]	
	N 31° 29.604' W 111° 16.726'	park, look back at building
Ruby	[Ruby topographic map]	
	N 31° 27.871' W 111° 14.302'	gate to townsite
	N 31° 27.675' W 111° 14.200'	in middle of townsite
	N 31° 28.038' W 111° 13.989'	viewpoint from Ruby Road
Hank and Yank Spring	[Ruby topographic map]	
	N 31° 25.946' W 111° 11.226'	turnoff to Sycamore Canyon
	N 31° 25.766' W 111° 11.452'	small adobe wall
Tubac	[Tubac topographic map]	
	N 31° 36.764' W 111° 03.098'	entrance to town and shops
	N 31° 36.952' W 111° 02.936'	entrance to cemetery
Harshaw	[Harshaw topographic map]	
	N 31° 28.071' W 110° 42.477'	at intersection into town (private)
Mowry	[Harshaw topographic map]	
	N 31° 25.506' W 110° 42.166'	intersection; north to mine
Washington Camp	[Harshaw topographic map]	
	N 31° 22.952' W 110° 41.503'	middle of town on road
Duquesne	[Duquesne topographic map]	
	N 31° 22.287' W 110° 41.150'	middle of town on road
Lochiel	[Lochiel topographic map]	
	N 31° 20.142' W 110° 37.451'	turnoff to former border station (private)

Sunnyside	[Huachuca Peak topographic map]	
	N 31° 26.061' W 110° 24.264'	townsite entrance (private)

Specific Directions: The road to Sunnyside is 17 miles northeast of Lochiel. Follow the signs from Lochiel directing you to Parker Canyon Lake. The turnoff that heads northeast into the townsite, which is 2 miles south of Parker Canyon Lake, is FR 228 and is marked for Sunnyside Canyon. One mile from the original turnoff, take the left fork where FR 4761 goes right and follow the main road for 2.2 miles beyond that fork. Do not take either the road marked to Ft. Huachuca or to Sunnyside Canyon but continue straight to the townsite. If you come from the north, Sunnyside is 32 miles south of Sonoita. FR 228 requires a high-clearance vehicle.

Salero	[Patagonia topographic map]	
	N 31° 34.486' W 110° 51.686'	park here; walk to hilltop ca. 200 yards east to view site
Alto	[Patagonia topographic map]	
	N 31° 37.236' W 110° 52.561'	at the post office ruins
Helvetia	[Helvetia topographic map]	
	N 31° 51.068' W 110° 48.506'	cemetery
	N 31° 51.486' W 110° 47.355'	turnoff; follow road east-northeasr to ruins
	N 31° 51.526' W 110° 47.213'	ruins

Specific Directions: From I-19 south of Tucson, take the Sahuarita Road exit (Exit 75). Go east for 2.6 miles to Santa Rita Road and turn south. That road turns to dirt and becomes FR 505, which heads southeast and eventually loops back around to the north. In 11.3 miles from Sahuarita Road, FR 505 passes the tiny Helvetia Cemetery on the west side of the road (Be on the lookout, as it is easy to miss.). Beyond the cemetery .8 of a mile is the entrance to Helvetia Ranch. Turn northeast on a road just beyond the ranch entrance and proceed .5 of a mile. A turnoff onto a four-wheel drive track going northeast takes you in .2 of a mile to the sparse adobe ruins of Helvetia. Under normal road conditions, a passenger car can travel all but the last .2 of a mile.

Greaterville	[Empire Ranch, Helvetia topos]	
	N 31° 45.847' W 110° 45.087'	gate to townsite (private)
	N 31° 45.880' W 110° 45.027'	cemetery (private)
Kentucky Camp	[Sonoita topographic map]	
	N 31° 44.867' W 110° 44.506'	gate; park nearby
	N 31° 44.678' W 110° 44.518'	townsite

Chapter Eight

Bisbee	[Bisbee topographic map]	
	N 31° 26.499' W 109° 54.933'	in front of post office
Lowell	[Bisbee topographic map]	
	N 31° 25.831' W 109° 53.655'	middle of shopping district
Warren	[Bisbee topographic map]	
	N 31° 24.821' W 109° 52.612'	middle of shopping district
Tombstone	[Tombstone topographic map]	
	N 31° 42.753' W 110° 03.991'	on Allen Street; town center
	N 31° 43.840' W 110° 06.202'	Schieffelin Monument
Charleston	[Fairbank topographic map]	
	N 31° 38.112' W 110° 10.612'	central Charleston
Millville	[Fairbank topographic map]	
	N 31° 38.306' W 110° 10.415'	at the base of smelter
Fairbank	[Fairbank topographic map]	
	N 31° 43.330' W 110° 11.308'	at cattle guard in front of store
Brunckow's Cabin	[Fairbank topographic map]	
	N 31° 38.559' W 110° 09.209'	within walls of "cabin" ruin
Fort Bowie	[Bowie Mtn. N. topographic map]	
	N 32° 09.403' W 109° 27.157'	parking lot; begin hike
	N 32° 08.660' W 109° 26.170'	flagpole on parade grounds
Dos Cabezas	[Dos Cabezas topographic map]	
	N 32° 10.507' W 109° 36.915'	on highway; mid-town
Cochise	[Cochise topographic map]	
	N 32° 06.837' W 109° 55.257'	in front of post office
Dragoon Spgs. Stage Station	[Knob Hill topographic map]	
	N 31° 59.861' W 110° 01.351'	in front of ruins
Pearce	[Pearce topographic map]	
	N 31° 54.308' W 109° 49.271'	in front of historic store
Courtland	[Turquoise Mtn. topographic map]	
	N 31° 45.848' W 109° 48.552'	southernmost buildings
	N 31° 46.223' W 109° 48.528'	Courtland jail
Gleeson	[Outlaw Mtn. topographic map]	
	N 31° 43.957' W 109° 49.772'	mid-town; near old saloon

Glossary of Mining Terms

adit: A nearly horizontal entrance to a mine.

assay: To determine the value of a sample of ore, in ounces per ton, by using a chemical evaluation.

charcoal kiln (or oven): A structure into which wood is placed and subjected to intense heat through controlled, slow burning. Charcoal is a longer lasting, more efficient wood fuel often used to power mills and smelters. If the kiln is used to convert coal to coke, it is called a "coke oven."

chloride: Usually refers to ores containing chloride of silver.

claim: A tract of land with defined boundaries that includes mineral rights extending downward from the surface.

diggings: Used in this book in the broadest sense as evidence of mining efforts, such as waste dumps, tailings, or placer workings. Technically, it refers specifically to placer mining.

grubstake: An advance of money, food, and/or supplies to a prospector in return for a share of any discoveries.

headframe: The vertical apparatus over a mine shaft that has cables to raise or lower a cage with miners or containers of ore; sometimes called a "gallows frame."

high-grading: The theft of rich ore, usually by a miner working for someone else who owns the mine.

ingot: A cast bar or block of a metal.

lode: A continuous mineral-bearing deposit or vein.

mill: A building in which rock is crushed to extricate minerals by one of several methods. If this is done by stamps (heavy hammers or pestles), it's a stamp mill. If by iron balls, it's a ball mill. The mill is usually constructed on the side of a hill to utilize its slope — hence, a gravity-fed mill.

mining district: An area of land described (usually for legal purposes) and designated as containing valuable minerals in paying amounts.

ore: A mineral of sufficient concentration, quantity, and value to be mined at a profit.

pan: To look for gold by washing earth, gravel, or sand, usually in a streambed.

placer: A waterborne deposit of sand or gravel containing heavier materials like gold that have been eroded from their original bedrock and concentrated as small particles that can be washed, or "panned," out.

prospect: Mineral workings of unproven value.

shaft: A vertical or nearly vertical opening into the earth for mining.

slag: The waste product of a smelter; hence, slag dumps.

smelter: A building or complex in which material is melted in order to separate impurities from pure metal.

tailings: Waste or refuse left after milling is complete; sometimes used more generally, although incorrectly, to indicate waste dumps.

tramway: An apparatus for moving materials such as ore, rock, or even supplies in buckets suspended from pulleys that run on a cable.

waste dump: Waste rock, not of sufficient value to warrant milling, that comes out of the mine; usually found immediately outside the mine entrance.

workings: A general term indicating any mining development.

Acknowledgments

For consistent, valuable historical assistance and advice: Dean Smith.

For field-work support: Suzanne Lawder, Mary Anne Stewart, Darryl Day, Janet Varney, Bill and June Porter, Tom Bartlett, Tim and Judy Phillips, Royce Kardinal, John and Roberta Crawford, Betty Rowe, Ralph and Joan Shelton, Charles J. Cook, Michael Moore.

For opening doors, files, photo albums, and memories: Tom Cleator (Cleator); John and Marge Osborne (Vulture); Charles and Jeri Robson (Robson's Mining World); Ruth Gaisford and A.J. and Linda Mac Farlane (Humbug); June L. Palmer and Charles A. Spezia (Clifton); Albert Jackman and Stan Christopher (Ruby); Jim MacDonald and Stacy Kroh (Kentucky Camp); Larry Ludwig (Fort Bowie); Elizabeth Fulton Husband and Lillie Harrington (Cochise).

For photographic advice: Mick Landau of Photographic Works Lab, Tucson.

For assistance with research of historical photographs, special thanks to: Heather Hatch and Don Bufkin, Tucson; Sue Abbey, Sharlot Hall Museum, Prescott; Lora Freed, Mohave County Historical Society, Kingman; Cheryl Taylor and Peg Darby, Desert Caballeros Western Museum, Wickenburg; Susie Sato and Kris Darnall, Arizona Historical Foundation, Tempe; Richard Pearce-Moses and Christine Marin, Hayden Library, Arizona State University, Tempe; Brenda McClurkin, Arizona State Library and Archives, Phoenix; John Drew, Scottsdale; Jeremy Rowe, Tempe; Melissa Keane, Tempe; James N. Price, San Diego, California; Dennis Casebier, Goffs, California; Teresa Salazar and Chris Ziegler, University of Arizona Library, Tucson; Megan Reid, Rio Colorado Division, Arizona Historical Society, Yuma; John Patterson, Yuma Crossing Foundation; and the staffs of the Bisbee Mining Museum, Bisbee; Clemenceau Heritage Museum, Cottonwood; Yuma Prison State Historic Park, Yuma; San Pedro Valley Arts and Historical Society, Benson; Blythe, California, Historical Society; and the Smithsonian Institution and Library of Congress, Washington D.C.

For map, p. 81: "Early History of Mining in Arizona, Acquisition of Mineral Rights 1539-1866" by John C. Lacy, in *History of Mining in Arizona*, Volume 1. Used with permission of the author and the Mining Foundation of the Southwest.